Gary Branson's
Home Repairs and Improvements on a Budget

To prevent accidents, keep safety in mind while you work. Use the safety guards installed on power equipment; they are for your protection. When working on power equipment, keep fingers away from saw blades, wear safety goggles to prevent injuries from flying wood chips and sawdust, wear headphones to protect your hearing, and consider installing a dust vacuum to reduce the amount of airborne dust in your woodshop. Don't wear loose clothing, such as neckties or shirt with loose sleeves, or jewelry, such as rings, necklaces or bracelets, when working on power equipment, and tie back long hair to prevent it from getting caught in your equipment.

The author and editors who compiled this book have tried to make all the contents as accurate as possible. Plans, illustrations, photographs and text have been carefully checked. All instructions, plans and projects should be carefully read, studied and understood before beginning construction. Due to the variability of local conditions, construction materials, skill levels, etc., neither the author nor Betterway Books assumes any responsibility for any accidents, injuries, damages or other losses incurred resulting from the material presented in this book.

METRIC CONVERSION CHART

TO CONVERT	TO	MULTIPLY BY
Inches	Centimeters	2.54
Centimeters	Inches	0.4
Feet	Centimeters	30.5
Centimeters	Feet	0.03
Yards	Meters	0.9
Meters	Yards	1.1
Sq. Inches	Sq. Centimeters	6.45
Sq. Centimeters	Sq. Inches	0.16
Sq. Feet	Sq. Meters	0.09
Sq. Meters	Sq. Feet	10.8
Sq. Yards	Sq. Meters	0.8
Sq. Meters	Sq. Yards	1.2
Pounds	Kilograms	0.45
Kilograms	Pounds	2.2
Ounces	Grams	28.4
Grams	Ounces	0.04

Gary Branson's
Home Repairs and Improvements on a Budget

BETTERWAY BOOKS

Cincinnati, Ohio

About the Author

Gary D. Branson was a building trades contractor for more than twenty years before starting a successful writing career. Formerly senior editor of *The Family Handyman* magazine, he now contributes to other how-to magazines. Gary is author of *The Complete Guide to Remodeling Your Basement*, *The Complete Guide to Lumber Yards and Home Centers*, *The Complete Guide to Recycling at Home*, *The Complete Guide to Barrier-Free Housing*, *The Complete Guide to Manufactured Housing*, *The Complete Guide to Floors, Walls and Ceilings*, and *The Complete Guide to Log and Cedar Homes*. He lives in Richfield, Minnesota.

Gary Branson's Home Repairs and Improvements on a Budget. Copyright © 1994 by Gary D. Branson. Printed and bound in the United States of America. All rights reserved. No part of this book may be reproduced in any form or by any electronic or mechanical means including information storage and retrieval systems without permission in writing from the publisher, except by a reviewer, who may quote brief passages in a review. Published by Betterway Books, an imprint of F&W Publications, Inc., 1507 Dana Avenue, Cincinnati, Ohio 45207. 1-800-289-0963. First edition.

98 97 96 95 94   5 4 3 2 1

Library of Congress Cataloging in Publication Data

Branson, Gary D.
    [Home repairs and improvements on a budget]
    Gary Branson's home repairs and improvements on a budget / by Gary D. Branson. — 1st ed.
        p.   cm.
    Includes index.
    ISBN 1-55870-338-1 (pbk.)
    1. Dwellings — Maintenance and repair — Amateurs' manuals. I. Title. II. Title: Home repairs and improvements on a budget.
TH 4817.3.B734 1994
643'.7 — dc20   94-14423
                                                                              CIP

Edited by Hilary Swinson
Cover and interior design by Brian Roeth

Betterway Books are available at special discounts for sales promotions, premiums and fund-raising use. Special editions or book excerpts can also be created to specification. For details contact: Special Sales Director, Betterway Books, 1507 Dana Avenue, Cincinnati, Ohio 45207.

Dedicated to my brother, Dean Branson.

TABLE OF CONTENTS

INTRODUCTION

During school vacations in my teens, my father took me out to work on his construction crew and taught me how to build. In one role or another I've spent my entire working life in the home-building business. For more than twenty-five years I was a contractor, working on new homes during the midwestern building season and remodeling houses in the winter off-season. Because of the diversity of the work, the remodeling business was especially good training. Rather than being limited to learning a single trade, remodeling gave me an opportunity to learn a wide variety of skills. These skills proved to be a valuable resource in my later occupation of writing home-repair advice.

In 1977 I took a job as technical editor for a home-repair magazine, *The Family Handyman*. I often wrote replies to the reader-response column called "Ask Handyman" and fielded many telephone calls from readers who sought help with home-repair problems. I also represented *The Family Handyman* and the Aerosol Packaging Council on radio shows — plus TV and newspaper interviews — in twenty-two cities, talking with thousands of homeowners.

Among the features I wrote during my ten years at the magazine was a series of fourteen articles called "The Whole House Repair Manual." Throughout those years of daily exposure to homeowners' questions, I conducted my own survey of the most common problems. This book is a sort of homecoming: For most of my adult life, I've been telling folks how to save money by maintaining and repairing their own homes. This book offers solutions to the most common repair and maintenance problems. I hope to have added something of value from my own experience.

HOW TO USE THIS BOOK

When writing a how-to book it's impossible to judge the experience and the abilities of each reader. There is the Dagwood type who bungles the simplest task and always ends up calling in a pro to fix his mistakes, and there are those who have a knack for hands-on work and can do anything. And there is every skill level between these two extremes. The reader alone must decide whether he or she is capable of doing a particular repair or maintenance task.

The book is a guide to the basic home maintenance and repair jobs. Most people respond to repair or maintenance instructions more readily if they understand the reasons for doing the job. I try to tell the reader not only *how* to do a particular job, but also *why* certain procedures are necessary. For example, caulking a crack between siding and a doorframe is important because the caulk keeps out rain that might enter the crack and cause peeling paint or rotted siding or trim. But the caulk also serves other purposes, such as keeping out dirt and insects and conserving home energy. These added benefits are mentioned to further encourage the reader to do the task.

The reader is given an informed estimate of the degree of difficulty of each project. If the do-it-yourselfer (DIYer) is given some instruction and has the right tools for the job, many home maintenance and repair jobs are within his or her ability, but there are some projects that usually or always should be left to the pros. I've read and reviewed a thousand books that lead homeowners toward areas the average amateur should never venture in. Some enthusiastic do-it-yourselfers may be convinced to tackle a job by such anyone-can-do-it claims, much to their future regret. I have talked to thousands of people and gotten a fair idea of the failure rate of certain projects and the ultimate cost of those failures. The most wasteful and expensive project possible results when the DIYer attempts to do it himself and fails, and then must pay a professional to first undo his mistakes and then complete the repair.

For example, many people have bathtubs with damaged finishes. In the past, the only solution was to tear out the tile and the wall materials, remove and replace the damaged tub, and then refinish the wall and install ceramic tile. This process cost the consumer thousands of dollars. Is there an alternative to removing the tub? There is: refinishing the bathtub with a new epoxy material. Are epoxy kits available for do-it-yourselfers? They are, but this is not a good do-it-yourself project. Why not? Because having a bathtub refinished by a pro costs around $300, as compared to a DIY kit that may cost $75 or more, so the potential savings is not great. But the most important reason for discouraging the homeowner from doing the job himself is the high failure rate for this project. In order for the epoxy paint to form a strong bond, you must clean the tub and remove the soap scum. The tub must be treated with very caustic and dangerous acids, acids that amateurs *never* should handle because of the chance of personal injury. Cleaning with a less-caustic cleaner may not remove all the soap residue, and the epoxy paint will peel. The high failure rate, coupled with the minimal possible savings,

determines that this job should be left to pros. Will some people still elect to try it? Of course, and I provide the information needed to do the job. It is only right to warn people, however, that experience dictates against success for the amateur.

There are many other tasks that should be left to professionals. Some of these are handled by simply excluding them from the book: For example, many people can do simple electrical repairs, such as replacing switches and receptacles, but most people are not competent to wire a new house.

To repeat the opening premise: The reader alone can assess his or her level of expertise for a given project. However, a further observation may be in order. As house prices have risen, an increasing number of buyers are hiring professional inspectors to assess the condition and code compliance of the houses. These inspectors are reporting more and more frequently that they find that many DIY projects must be professionally redone because they have been poorly executed or because they do not meet building codes. For any legally contested repair, a contractor will be required to prove that he executed the project in a *workmanlike manner*, and that is the standard to which an inspector will hold DIY repairs. This is not to discourage DIY activity, but to encourage each reader to increase his or her expertise through further study and to exercise common sense when deciding whether to hire a professional or do the job himself.

CHAPTER 1

PAINTING

Painting is the one maintenance job that most of us feel competent to tackle. Surveys have shown that 95 percent of homeowners do at least some of their own painting. Over the past few decades advances in paint chemistry have produced water-based latex paints that give off less objectionable odor, dry with less pollution, and clean up with water rather than chemical solvents. New developments in painting tools have resulted in such advances as airless paint sprayers, power paint rollers, brushes with man-made bristles and paint pads. Still, a large percentage of consumer questions about painting concern the subject of paint failure. In this chapter I will provide dozens of professional painting tips that will make both interior and exterior painting chores easier, and will also ensure that your paint jobs yield all the beauty and protection your paint products were designed to deliver.

EXTERIOR PAINTING

Preparation

The first step in this process, even before washing your house to clean it for painting, is to remove any old or cracked caulk. Cracked caulk can let water enter between and behind building components. This can cause wood rot or failed paint. Apply new caulk — either acrylic latex or silicone — to any cracks where two fixed (nonmoving) building materials meet. This will seal all cracks so water can't penetrate behind siding and/or trim. An added benefit of caulk-

To prevent water from entering cracks between siding and trim, clean and recaulk all cracks before power washing siding.

Photo courtesy DAP Inc.

ing is better energy conservation and consequently lower utility bills.

Preparation is the most important part of painting. Use a deck cleaner such as Dekswood (made by The Flood Company), or trisodium phosphate (TSP) to

Power wash the entire house before painting. Wash roof overhangs and porches carefully to remove accumulated grime.

clean all surfaces to be painted. Paint won't stick to surfaces that are dirty, mildewed or badly chalked. To ensure better adhesion of the new paint, use sandpaper to break the film or surface on high-gloss paint. Set (drive slightly below the surface) and fill popped siding nails, sand or scrape away peeling paint, and use a power washer to blast away grime.

Surfaces that are not regularly washed by rain can become very dirty and may require special cleaning attention. These unwashed areas may include soffits, roof overhangs and porch ceilings, along with siding that is protected by porches or awnings. Use a stiff scrub brush and deck cleaner or TSP to clean these protected areas.

Test any discolored areas to see whether the stains are dirt or mildew. Simple washing will remove dirt, but water will not remove mildew. Treat the stained area with a 50-50 solution of water and chlorine bleach to kill the mildew spores. Mildew on siding often results when the siding is constantly in the shade and does not dry. Sunlight and moving air will help keep the siding dry and free of future mildew growth, so trim away any trees or shrubs to open up the siding to sunlight and to air circulation.

Remove clinging vines before painting. Use pruning shears to clip the vines away. You may also want to use a propane torch to very carefully burn away remaining tendrils.

Use plastic or canvas drop cloths to cover and protect walks, drives and shrubbery from spills and spatters. Professional painters prefer canvas drop cloths to plastic because canvas drops are not slippery to walk on, they are heavy enough so they do not become wind-blown, and they absorb spills so the paint does not smear onto other surfaces. Paint will lie wet on plastic covers and can make a mess on siding, shrubs or other objects if the plastic covers are not moved carefully.

Use pruning shears to remove vines from masonry or siding.

Buying Paint

Measure the house carefully, and take the measurements with you to your paint dealer. Try to estimate paint needs accurately, so you will not have to run back for extra paint. By the same token, you do not want to buy more than you need. Paint dealers usually will not accept the return of custom-mixed colors, so you will be stuck with any unused paint.

Choose your color carefully. Consider the colors of other house components that cannot be changed, such as roofing, brick or masonry chimneys or fireplaces, and landscaping. Drive through an area of houses similar to your own and check out colors that are especially attractive. Paint colors can have a great impact on your home's curb appeal.

Take a color photo of your house and bring it to the paint dealer so he can help with your color choice. For example, Victo-

rian houses look best when painted in traditional colors such as gray, blue, white and yellow. Keep in mind that light colors make a house look larger, while dark colors make a house look smaller. Also consider the color of houses nearby and avoid copycat or clashing colors.

There should be no question about the kind of paint to buy: By a very wide margin homeowners now choose latex over oil-based paints. Latex paint is more forgiving in application because it dries more quickly than alkyd (oil), so dirt and insects do not get into the paint; you can apply latex paint when there is a slight dew on the siding; and it is environmentally better because water is used rather than chemicals for thinning and cleanup.

Compared to the work of preparation and application, the cost of the paint is a small part of the project. Avoid ''bargain'' or discount paints. Buy the best quality

Small tendrils left from vines can be removed with a propane torch. To prevent unwanted combustion when burning vines off wood siding, do not leave the flame in one place for a long time and keep a garden hose handy to wet down the siding as soon as the tendrils are burned off.

paint you can find. For a bargain price, shop for name-brand paints at sale time, usually around midsummer. Major sales come just after the Fourth of July and again in the fall.

When to Paint

Read — and follow — the paint label directions. This means no painting when temperatures are below 50° F (10° C) or above 90° F (32° C). Don't paint on windy days, when wind may blow insects or dirt into the paint or dry the paint prematurely. Latex paints are more forgiving than oil-based paints for painting damp surfaces, but it's best not to paint when it is too wet or humid.

The best time to paint the exterior of your house is in late spring or early summer, before plant pollen blows, before the earth gets dusty, and before bugs hatch to mar wet paint. Paint will also spread more easily, and you will be more comfortable if work is done before summer temperatures rise.

Tools and Techniques

Choose the right tool for the job. Use a paint roller on large surfaces or wide-lap siding; use a brush to paint narrow-lap siding or trim. Use an airless sprayer to paint rough surfaces, such as masonry or rough-sawn wood siding. Tell the paint dealer what types of surfaces you'll be painting

To get the best results choose the right tool for the job. Use a long-nap roller to paint chain-link fencing.

An airless paint sprayer is the best tool for painting rough or irregular surfaces. For very large paint jobs, you can rent larger sprayers.

and ask him to help select the proper tools for the job.

What is the right size paintbrush to use? That depends on two things: the size of the paint job, and the size of the painter. Use the widest brush you can comfortably handle. You will find that using a brush 4″ wide or larger can become very tiring un-

less you are a bodybuilder. Use a tool that you will be able to handle for hours without fatigue.

Wear protective equipment. A dust mask is fine for ordinary sanding, but choose an OSHA-approved paint mask for spray painting or when working with oil-based or epoxy paints. Wear goggles for eye protection and a paint hat to help keep dirt and paint out of your hair and eyes.

Wear proper clothes. Tough white canvas painter's pants are snag-resistant and will soak up spilled paint before it can reach your skin. Multiple tool pockets on the pants will hold needed tools while leaving your hands free for working or climbing ladders.

Practice good ladder safety. Check the load limits listed on the ladder label. Remember that the ladder's load will include the combined weight of the painter, the materials and the tools. Keep ladders away from power lines, particularly metal ladders, which conduct electricity.

Don't overthin paint. Paint goes on easiest and lasts longest when it is applied as formulated. Paint that is too thin will run, sag, drip and spatter, and protective quali-

Use a paintbrush or pad to paint smooth, flat surfaces such as narrow-lap siding.

ties may be sacrificed. Most manufacturers recommend that you limit thinning to not more than one pint of water per gallon of paint to ensure durability.

Measure the area covered as you apply the paint and make sure that the *spread rate* (the recommended coverage) is not exceeded. Most paints recommend a spread rate of 350-400 square feet per gallon on smooth, previously painted surfaces. But be aware that the coverage can depend on the surface to be painted. Trying to extend the coverage by thinning—or excessive rolling—will result in a paint film that is too thin and therefore will fail prematurely.

There are often slight color shifts between batches of paint. To avoid seeing color shifts in the finished paint job, pour several gallons of paint into a plastic five-gallon pail and mix the paint thoroughly. This professional technique is called *boxing* the paint. You should mix enough paint together to easily cover one entire side of the house. Color shifts or changes will not be noticeable if they occur at the outside corners where two walls meet.

Don't carry a full gallon can up a ladder. If you spill a full gallon of paint you'll make

a terrible mess. Instead, use a can opener to remove the rim from a one-gallon paint pail; use this rimless pail as a work pail. Pour the paint into the work pail—no more than one quart at a time—and work from this partial pail. You'll find carrying the smaller quantity of paint is much less tiring, and if you spill the paint you won't

To remove chalked paint, clean the siding with deck cleaner.

have such a big mess to clean up.

If your house has stucco siding, ask your paint dealer or a stucco contractor whether you should paint the stucco or *redash* it (apply a new coat of stucco rather than paint over the old stucco). In northern climates with severe temperature extremes painted stucco often peels, so contractors usually redash stucco rather than painting it. If you decide to paint the stucco ask your paint dealer to recommend a quality acrylic latex masonry paint for the job. For painting aluminum, unpainted wood or log siding see chapter seven, "Exterior," for further advice.

To extend the life of your paint job, inspect the exterior each spring; recaulk, scrape and touch up paint as required to keep the paint film clean and intact. Don't wait until the entire house needs repainting to correct any problems. Remember that polluted air may carry contaminants that can dull or damage the painted surface. Power wash your house each spring to remove the accumulated dirt and grime and to keep that just-painted look.

Exterior Painting Checklist

• Wash all surfaces to be painted and scrape peeling paint.

• Treat mildewed areas with a chlorine bleach/water solution.

• Estimate paint needs accurately.

• Use a roller for large surfaces; a brush for narrow siding and trim; an airless sprayer for masonry or rough-sawn wood siding.

• Don't overthin paint or exceed the recommended spread rate.

• Inspect the exterior every spring and plan to touch up as needed.

INTERIOR PAINTING

Because painting is one of the most popular do-it-yourself chores, most people think they know how to paint. But the pros know that there is a right way to do everything, and many paint jobs are botched by a lack of expertise. To help you with your next interior paint job, check the following list of tips to see whether you are following good painting procedures.

Tools

Select the right tool for the job. A tapered sash brush is better than a square-end brush for cutting the line between the window sash and glass. A medium- to long-nap paint roller will do a better job than a short-nap roller when painting a wall or ceiling, even when painting over an existing coat of flat paint. The longer nap of the roller will hold more paint, and will lay paint on the wall without pressure, resulting in a finish coat with fewer lap marks and skips, or *holidays*, in the paint. Ask the paint salesman to help you select the right tools for your job. Using worn-out brushes and half-cleaned paint rollers will spoil the paint job, no matter how good the paint product you use.

Don't work with a makeshift scaffold. Using a rickety ladder, a chair or a kitchen stool as a work scaffold can be tiring at best, and at worst you could suffer a dangerous fall. Check the load rating listed on the ladder label. Buy a sturdy commercial ladder that is capable of supporting not only your weight, but also the weight of tools and materials.

Choosing Paint

Use latex paint on most interior surfaces. Keep in mind that most pros still prefer using alkyd or oil-based paints on furniture, woodwork and cabinets. Doors and drawers on furniture and cabinets are likely to stick if painted with latex paint. Flat pieces, like bookshelves, can also retain a sticky film if finished with latex. Handprints are harder to clean from surfaces with latex finishes.

Avoid bargain paint. At best, you might save only a few dollars per gallon at a cost

of a substandard job. Compared to job preparation, labor and cleanup, the cost of the paint is a small item. Don't spend all that time and energy applying a paint product that won't last.

Before choosing a paint color, spend time considering the impact that color can have on the room. Small paint samples may not show you how the paint will look on a large wall. For a better idea of the prospective paint's effect, tape four or more paint chips from the paint store together to make a larger sample. Leave the sample chip in the room and examine it in varying natural and artificial lighting — early morning, late afternoon and evening light. If you like the color, have the paint store mix a quart of it. Paint one wall, and then examine the color again at various times of the day and night. Color shifts dramatically as lighting changes, so consider the color carefully in a variety of lights before painting the entire room.

Application

To be sure that the paint you choose will cover, hide and provide durability, follow the label directions carefully. Apply the paint at the spread rate recommended on the label. If the label recommends the paint to cover only 350 square feet, don't try to stretch the coverage to 450 square feet. The resulting thin paint film won't cover or last as well as the thicker film produced by the recommended spread rate.

If you are painting over a same or similar color, blue over blue, for example, you might get by with one coat. But for most paint jobs, especially if you are changing the color of the room, it's easier and wiser to plan on applying two coats for complete coverage and better durability.

Environmental Considerations

Latex paints have less environmental impact than alkyd (oil) paints, and have the added advantage of using water for thinning and cleanup. Leftover paints can be difficult to dispose of, so measure rooms to be painted carefully and buy just enough paint to do the job. If you have a bit of paint left after the job, use it to paint a closet or give one wall an extra coat. Never pour old paint down the drain or into a stream.

How else can you get rid of leftover paint? Donate it to groups that work with the elderly or poor, give it away to theater groups to be used for painting stage sets or props, or contact your trash service to see if they can take care of disposal. Some paint stores will also dispose of leftover paint for you.

Preparation for Painting

It is frustrating and time-consuming to repeatedly move furniture or other objects from the work area. Stack and cover large furniture items in the middle of the room. Remove mirrors and pictures from the walls. Remove all curtains, drapes and hardware from the windows.

To protect floors from spills you can cover small areas with old newspapers or plastic sheets. If you do much painting, however, it is best to invest in canvas painter's tarps to protect the floors. Canvas tarps, or drop cloths, are heavy enough to stay in place; they cannot be picked up and carried on your feet as plastic coverings can. Paint spills soak into the canvas and will not be picked up on your shoes and tracked through the house. Buy several 9′ × 12′ canvas tarps; use them individually in bedrooms or in multiples to cover larger living room floors.

Surface Preparation

The most important part of painting is surface preparation. All surfaces to be painted, whether walls, ceilings or woodwork, must be clean and dust-free, with no loose or peeling paint. If the surface to be painted is washable use a strong detergent, such as Spic 'N Span or TSP, to clean all dirt and grease away.

If stains are present on walls or ceilings, make the indicated repairs to prevent stains from reappearing. Repair leaking pipes or the roof before trying to deal with water stains. If the stain is from latex paint spatters, adhesive from "stick-ons," colored markers or crayons use a cleaning product, such as Goof Off, to remove the stain rather than trying to cover it with paint. If you can't remove the stain you can cover and seal it with a coat of shellac sealer such as BIN. Use shellac sealer or a comparable product for priming and sealing smoke-damaged walls or ceilings, or for sealing difficult-to-paint surfaces such as tempered hardboard or high-gloss paint.

Making Needed Repairs

No matter how fresh the paint job, unfilled cracks between trim or moldings and wall or ceilings will always look dirty. To get a clean, professional-looking job, fill cracks with a paintable acrylic latex caulk and smooth it with a wet fingertip.

Structural cracks are cracks caused by movement of the structure; they will reopen if simply filled with spackle. Treat all cracks as structural cracks (not hairline or minor cracks). Use fiber wallboard tape and taping compound to tape and finish the cracks. Apply a coat of premixed taping compound over the crack, lay the wallboard tape in the compound, and then smooth the tape with a 6-inch wide taping knife. When the tape is dry use a taping knife to wipe a thin coat of wallboard compound over the tape; let this first covercoat dry and apply a second thin coat of compound. Use a wet sponge or fine sandpaper to smooth the repair area. Apply a coat of primer over the repair and repaint the wall. **Tip:** If there are many cracks, don't spot prime. Prime the entire wall or ceiling. Many spot-primed areas may yield a polka-dot look to the finish paint.

Old methods of patching holes in walls or ceilings were made obsolete by the invention of peel-and-stick patches or *bandages*. The patches consist of a metal foil base covered by a fiber glass mesh backing. The fiber glass mesh has an adhesive coat-

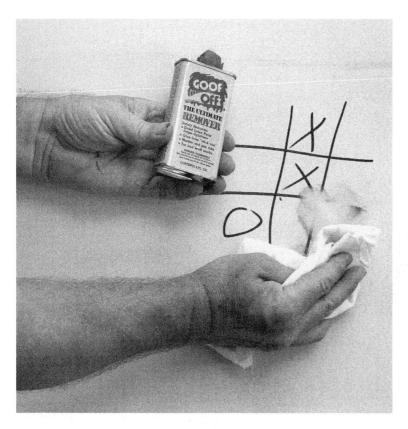

Before painting, use a cleaner such as Goof-Off to remove marks from crayons or permanent marker.

Cover stubborn stains such as rust or oil with a shellac sealer.

ing so the patch can be pressed into place over holes up to 6 inches in diameter—larger holes must be repaired using old patching methods. Cover and smooth the patch with coats of spackle or premixed wallboard cement. Using this type of patch, you can easily patch and paint the same day, with no waiting for deep plaster patches to dry. (For patching instructions see chapter two, "Interior.")

To reduce the mess and cleanup of painting repairs, avoid procedures that produce dust. Do not use powder-type patch products (plaster or wallboard cement) that require mixing and create dust. Instead, use only premixed patching materials. To avoid sanding old paint or new patches, use a liquid paint deglosser—such as Kleen Strip's No Sand—or a strong solution of TSP to dull glossy paint finishes. Use a wallboard wet sander (a wet sponge with an abrasive nylon cover) to smooth patches over holes or cracks, avoiding the dust from sandpaper.

Priming

How do you decide when to prime before painting? When in doubt, always prime the surface. Small repair areas can be spot primed, but if the repair areas are extensive, covering half or more of the total wall or ceiling area, it's best to prime the entire surface.

Use latex primers over most clean wall or ceiling surfaces. Use alkyd (oil) primers on surfaces that are excessively soiled by grease, smoke (cooking and/or fireplace) or nicotine. For really tough stains such as yellowed water stains, rust, or smoke or grease from a house fire, use a shellac base sealer.

Painting Ceilings

When painting ceilings, use lightweight 1- or 2-mil-thick, 8-foot-wide plastic sheets to cover furniture and walls from floor to ceiling. Use 2-inch-wide masking tape to hold the plastic in place, or buy plastic coverings such as Tape 'N Drape that have a convenient adhesive edge already attached.

Textured ceilings are hard to paint, because they are both rough and highly absorbent. The blotter-like absorbency tends to suck up the paint so that the painted surface shows roller marks and uneven gloss or sheen. Because the texture paint is applied by spraying with air equipment, using techniques that may be difficult for the amateur to master, consider calling a professional to respray the ceilings when it's time to redecorate. To find a pro look in the Yellow Pages under "Dry Wall Contractors."

If you decide to tackle a spray-textured ceiling yourself, use a long-nap paint roller to apply alkyd (oil base) sealer over the entire ceiling. Let the sealer dry for twenty-four hours, then finish off with a roller-applied topcoat of a flat acrylic latex ceiling paint.

Remove light fixtures before painting the ceiling. Not only is it easier to paint with the fixture out of the way, but you should paint right up to the edge of the electrical box to avoid leaving an unpainted ring around the box. This way, if you decide to replace the light fixture at a later date, you won't have to repaint the ceiling to get rid of the ring around the light box.

Techniques and Tips

When painting around glass panes in windows or doors, it's better to cut the line with a brush rather than trying to use masking tape on the glass. The paint should overlap the glass by about 1/8 inch to provide a moisture seal between the glass and the sash or frame. Masking the glass with tape interferes with getting the needed seal between the glass and sash. With a bit of practice you can learn to cut a straight line using a good sash brush.

When you do use masking tape be sure to wipe the surface to be taped free of dirt so the tape will stick. Apply the tape to the surface, and then use the tip end of a putty knife to apply pressure to the edge of the tape. This will ensure that the edge is firmly stuck down so paint cannot seep under the tape. Do not leave masking tape in place when you have finished painting; it will be difficult to remove once the paint dries. Remove the tape as soon as the paint is too dry to run. Check for runs, and clean them up before the paint has dried and is hard to remove.

It is much easier to remove cabinet hardware than to try to paint around it. If you will be painting cabinets or furniture remove all the hardware — door pulls, hinges and catches — before starting to paint. Place the hardware in a gallon plastic pail as you remove it, and use a separate container for each room so you can easily replace the hardware after painting. Also remove all electrical outlet covers, registers and ceiling light fixtures to avoid getting paint on them.

Older varnished woodwork may appear to need refinishing. Actually, the woodwork may be darkened with years of accumulated grease and grime. Try cleaning older varnished woodwork (trim, cabinets, moldings) with odorless mineral spirits to remove accumulated wax and dirt. Once it is cleaned you may be surprised to find the woodwork looks like new and does not need painting.

After painting with latex paints use warm soapy water to clean brushes and rollers. Invest in a paint spinner, which costs about $10 and will get tools much cleaner than ordinary washing. The spinner tool has a ratcheted shaft like a child's toy top. To use the spinner, slip the roller over the spinner body, or fit the brush handle in the spinner slot, and pump the handle rapidly to fling the paint particles out of the tool via centrifugal force. Hold the tool inside a five-gallon pail while spinning to avoid spattering yourself.

When you've finished painting, clip the brand name and color from the paint label and paste the information on the back side of a light-switch cover so that you or a future owner can quickly retrieve the brand and color of paint for future decorating

needs. Better still, keep a diary of all home decorating and repairs. List the products purchased, repairs needed and dates of repairs or replacement. Use the diary as a reference as long as you own the house, and when you sell, pass the maintenance diary to the new owner: it will be a much-appreciated housewarming gift.

Use a plastic snap-on tray, available from paint dealers, to catch drips and prevent unnecessary cleanup chores.

Interior Painting Checklist

• Use the right tools: medium- to long-nap roller for walls and ceilings; tapered sash brush for window trim.

• Choose paint color carefully; examine it in various lighting conditions before buying.

• Apply paint at recommended spread rate.

• Clean and remove dust from all surfaces; remove stains, or seal with shellac sealer.

• Fill small cracks; tape structural cracks

This tool spins a brush or roller clean by centrifugal force. Hold the spinner tool inside a plastic pail to catch the spatters.

as you would wallboard joints.

- Prime any areas that need it.
- Use a paint spinner to get brushes and rollers really clean.

PEELING PAINT

Perhaps the most common homeowner complaint is paint that fails or peels. The experienced painter can, with a little detective work, determine the cause of peeling paint and cure the problem so it does not recur. Following is a list of common points where paint commonly fails, the cause of the peeling, and how to prevent and cure the problem.

Window and Door Trim

Cause

Moisture seeks its own level. When moisture levels build indoors and outside humidity drops as air becomes colder in winter, the interior moisture is under natural pressure to escape to the drier air outside. It follows the path of least resistance: Moisture escapes through the siding on older houses that have no vapor barriers, and through the areas around the window and door openings on sealed modern houses, or stucco or brick houses.

Cure

Because you are fighting nature and trying to block the path of least resistance, it is very difficult to stop moisture migration through window and door trim. One step is to reduce moisture levels inside houses where excess moisture is a problem. Try to hold indoor humidity levels at 30 to 40 percent. Use a humidifier or dehumidifier depending on the problem—too little or too much moisture. Then change the paint on the trim, removing all the old failing paint down to bare wood. Because latex paint will permit moisture to pass through more readily than alkyd paint will, it's best to recoat the trim with latex paint. You can also apply a couple of coats of a paint conditioner, such as Penetrol, to the bare trim and then topcoat with an alkyd paint thinned with the same conditioner.

Prevention

When remodeling or building buy windows that have prefinished aluminum or vinyl cladding (overlay). These units are almost maintenance-free—almost, because no finish lasts forever without painting. But you should get twenty years or more of paint-free maintenance, and you will also have less peeling and paint problems on the aluminum or vinyl even after you finally have to paint, because moisture cannot penetrate from the backside and attack the paint film.

Cover any surface
you don't want
painted to avoid
roller spatters.
Heavy-bodied ma-
terials such as tex-
ture paints are es-
pecially prone to
splattering.

Soffits and Porch Ceilings

Enclosed soffits (sometimes called roof overhangs or eaves) and porch ceilings often have peeling paint. There are two common causes for peeling paint.

Cause

The first cause of peeling problems is lack of air transfer between the soffits or ceilings and the attic vents. Moisture that is trapped in these areas cannot easily exit and will migrate through the unpainted backside of the plywood or board finish, causing the paint on the surface to peel.

Cure

Install extra vents in the soffits and porch ceilings.

Cause

The other cause of peeling paint is failure to properly clean the underside of the soffits or porch ceiling. Painted areas that are washed by rain are periodically cleaned, so grime and oxidized paint are washed away.

Cure

Because rain does not wash these protected areas, you must take extra care in cleaning them before painting.

Porch Posts

Wooden porch posts that support a roof or safety railing, and sit upon a concrete or wood deck, often have peeling paint at their bases.

Cause

Peeling posts result when rain or snowmelt runs under the ends of the posts and enters upward through the unpainted wood grain. The moisture migrates to the outside paint film on the post, where it lifts the paint, causing it to peel.

Cure

If the wood in the post base is not rotted, scrape or burn the peeling paint away, using a paint scraper and a heat gun. Caulk the crack between the porch post end and the wood or concrete floor to prevent moisture from penetrating the area in the future. Then repaint the post using a quality acrylic latex paint. Periodically inspect the crack between the post end and the deck to be sure the caulk is intact.

Prevention

When building a deck or porch project, always seal and paint the ends of posts to protect against moisture penetration. Also, use metal post bases to connect the posts to the deck or floor. These metal post bases hold the bottom end of the posts slightly above the deck, so the post end and deck will not be in direct contact and water will not be trapped between the post end and the deck.

Siding on Gables

Suppose your house has gable ends: The siding paint on the finished first floor is in good shape, but the paint is peeling on the gable siding at the attic level, even though there are small louvered vents at each gable end.

Cause

Moisture from the living space of the house passes through the ceilings into the attic. Although there are small gable vents, they are not sufficient to prevent a buildup of moisture in the attic space. The moisture seeks its own level: In cold weather the interior moisture tries to pass to the outside and equalize with the relatively dry outside air. The moisture can penetrate the unpainted backside of the siding but is stopped by the paint film until it raises the paint, causing widespread peeling.

Cure

The only cures for moisture migration are (1) to retard the migration or entry of moisture into the attic by providing a vapor barrier in the ceiling, or (2) to increase the amount of ventilation to provide a path for the moisture to exit. To stop paint peeling on the gable siding, apply a coat of alkyd (oil base) sealer or paint to all the ceilings in your house. This oil paint will provide a vapor barrier to reduce moisture passage through the ceiling and into the attic. If you prefer a latex finish paint or spray texture for ceilings, apply an alkyd primer and then topcoat with the finish of your choice. Next, increase the amount of attic ventilation to remove excess moisture. The small gable vents normally installed in the past were too small to exhaust all the attic moisture. Install either more vents, larger vents or power vents to force moisture to exit via exhaust fans.

Prevention

Note that many building code requirements are *minimum* requirements, and may not be sufficient for the job. All the houses with attic moisture problems — as well as all the houses with wet basements — and all the underinsulated houses in the U.S. were code-approved by a building inspector. It costs very little to *exceed* the code requirements with extra vents or thicker insulation at the time of construction.

Detached Garages

Quite often, paint will peel on detached garages that are clad with wood siding.

Cause

The reason paint peels, as with house siding, is that there is no barrier on the inside of the building to stop moisture from migrating through the unpainted back and then lifting or peeling the paint on the outside surface.

Cure

To reduce peeling, spray a coat of clear wood sealer on the exposed bare wood siding on the interior of the garage. Some of the clear sealers, like Thompson's Water

Seal, have a water-like viscosity and can be sprayed through an ordinary pump-type garden sprayer. For other materials you may have to rent an airless sprayer: Check the label directions for application instructions.

Prevention

When building a garage or other outbuilding, use preprimed wood or composition siding, or aluminum or vinyl siding that is not affected by moisture.

Other Peeling Problems

The above mentioned are some of the more common situations where paint may peel, but there are numerous other such areas. For example, paint will often peel if it is directly in the path of steam being exhausted from a clothes dryer exhaust vent, or if water enters the ends of siding boards where the unpainted siding butts against window or door trim or against another piece of siding. The cures would be to redirect the steam from the dryer exhaust vent so the steam does not blow against the siding, or to caulk any cracks where two building materials meet, as when siding ends meet against window or door trim, so water or moisture cannot enter. The key is to not just settle for the fact that the paint will peel again, no matter what you do. There is a solution for most paint peeling problems, and you should find and implement the solution before repainting. If, after examination, you can't figure out why you have a peeling problem, ask the experts at your local paint store, or call a painting contractor and solicit his or her advice.

Peeling Paint Checklist

- Reduce indoor moisture levels if they are excessive.
- Install extra vents in soffits or porch ceilings.
- Put a vapor barrier in the ceiling and/or increase ventilation.
- Use materials such as aluminum-clad windows that are not affected by moisture for new/remodeling construction.

CHAPTER 2

INTERIOR

The systems, appliances, features — almost every aspect of your home — can fall apart if you don't establish a regular maintenance schedule. Neglected repairs become worse, more expensive and possibly dangerous. To extend the life and service of house components, save the owner's manuals for all home appliances and equipment, and perform maintenance as directed. Put together a tool kit and periodically make the rounds through the house, following the items covered in this chapter to check room by room for common interior maintenance and repair problems that may materialize.

WALLS AND CEILINGS
Repairing Plaster

Plaster is an age-old building material. It consists of three layers: a base of lath, which may be wood, rock or wire (metal) lath; a first or brown coat of plaster; and a finish or lime coat of finish plaster. Plaster is applied as a plastic material that can be built to almost any desired thickness or troweled to any shape. By increasing the thickness of plaster, one can produce a wall or ceiling surface that will meet almost any criteria for strength, soundproofing or fireproofing.

One problem with plaster is that it is monolithic, meaning that it is formed as a single, brittle covering over the top of the lath. When a wood-framed building settles, the wood shrinks, and stress builds up on the plaster. Because the plaster is brittle, like glass, it will crack when put under stress — i.e., when any twisting motion is applied during settling of the house. These cracks are called *structural cracks*, because they are caused by movement within the framing structure. This cracking of the plaster occurs most often at points where the shrinking framing lumber in the walls or ceilings moves in opposite directions: at corners where walls meet other walls, where walls meet ceilings, or where any opening (such as a door, window or archway) is cut into the wall or ceiling.

Because structural cracks are caused by

Use a nonshrinking plaster patcher, such as USG's Plaster Wall Patch, for filling holes or large cracks.

Photo courtesy USG.

movement of the structure, these cracks are difficult to repair. You cannot successfully repair them by putting brittle patching materials — such as patch plaster or spackle — into the crack. Brittle patches will re-crack when the structure moves again, usually as temperatures and humidity levels change with the seasons.

To patch structural cracks, tape and finish the cracks just as you would tape the joints in wallboard. Use paper tape, not fiber glass, to reinforce the joints. After taping the cracks, trowel a thin coat of taping compound over the tape and let dry. Then apply a second coat over the tape, wet-sand with a sponge or wallboard wet-sander, and spot prime the repairs. If there are extensive repairs to the wall or ceiling, prime the entire area.

Tiny random cracks in plaster, sometimes called *hairline cracks*, can be patched by filling them with spackle. If you are in doubt about whether a crack is hairline or structural, always treat the crack as structural, and tape and finish as above. For hairline cracks, buy ready-mix spackle and apply it with an appropriate tool: Use the smallest patching tool that will span the patch area in order to limit the size of the patch. You will find that smaller patch areas are easier to conceal with paint: Patches that are done with large trowels and spread over large areas will be hard to cover with paint when decorating. Smooth any patch, whether on plaster or wallboard, with a wet sponge or wallboard wet-sander to avoid the mess and dust generated by using sandpaper.

Patching Holes in Plaster

Sometimes plaster can fail, leaving a hole down to the lath. This can be caused by water damage (most often on ceilings) or by the impact of a blow (usually on walls). If a hole in plaster is caused by water damage, from a leaking pipe or a roof leak, for example, be sure to repair the leak before repairing the plaster. Any further exposure to water will cause the plaster to fail again.

Fill small cracks and nail holes with a fast-setting patcher such as UGL's 222 Lite.

Photo courtesy UGL.

Plaster can fail between the lath and brown (first) coat, or between the brown coat and finish, or lime, coat. If the failure is just in the surface coat you can remove the loose plaster and fill the shallow hole with any type of patching compound — taping compound or patch plaster. Be aware that taping compound shrinks more than patch plaster as it dries, so it requires extra coats of taping compound to fill the patch level. To patch with fewer coats, use patch plaster, which is a chemical-set material as opposed to an air-dry material such as wallboard taping compound, which has greater shrinkage.

A major problem with patch plaster is failure of the patch plaster to bond with the old plaster and the lath. To ensure getting a firm bond between the damaged plaster and the new patch, use a paintbrush to apply a coat of concrete bonding liquid to the lath and to the edges of the old plaster around the hole. Then fill the hole with patching plaster and allow it to set (plaster hardens, or *sets*, chemically, as opposed to wallboard taping compound which air *dries*). The bonding liquid will serve to bond both the old and new plaster and the plaster and lath together.

If plaster is old or has a wood lath base

To avoid future cracking, patch plaster cracks with reinforcing wallboard tape and compound.

Repairing Cracked Ceilings

If ceilings are cracked or buckled over wide areas, the plaster is probably failing. Not only can this be a lot of work (and expense) to repair, but gravity is also working against you. Badly deteriorated plaster can collapse without warning, damaging furnishings or injuring people below. If ceiling plaster is sagging, you must move quickly to avoid possible damage from collapse.

If a plaster ceiling is damaged there are three possible courses. After performing the test of pressing the plaster to see if it is sound, the first possibility is to repair the plaster. As suggested above, treat all cracks in plaster as structural, and tape and finish them as you would tape and finish the joints in wallboard.

If the plaster is loose, or if large areas have already failed and there are many holes in the plaster, you must cover the plaster over with wallboard. If the ceiling is generally flat and the plaster damaged but still tight to the lath, you can apply a layer of ½-inch thick wallboard directly over the old plaster. To apply wallboard over plaster you must first locate the ceiling joists. You can do this by going into the attic and driving a nail or drilling a hole into the ceiling on the sides of the ceiling joists. If the ceiling is closed and not accessible from above, as with a two-story house, you can probe with a hammer and a 16d nail, or with a drill, from the finished side of the ceiling. Once you have found one joist you can measure and locate all the others. In older houses the ceiling joist spacing will be sixteen inches on center (on center means from the center of one joist or stud to the center of the next joist or stud): Some newer houses may have joists or trusses spaced 24 inches on center. Use a wallboard screw gun and long wallboard screws to attach the wallboard to the ceiling. Be sure screws are long enough to penetrate through the plaster and lath and into the ceiling joists. This means using 2½- or 3-inch long screws to penetrate through ½-inch wallboard, ¾-

(pre-World War II construction) and has multiple cracks or holes, it may be coming loose from the lath. Wood lath was nailed on with a ¼-inch space between laths, so that plaster could sag between the lath and lock, or *key*, the plaster to the wood. As the plaster ages the keys break off and the plaster covering loosens from the lath and eventually fails. Plaster that is still keyed tightly to the lath can be successfully repaired, but if key loss occurs over a wide area the useful life of the plaster is ended and the only cure is complete removal or coverup.

To check plaster strength and viability, push firmly with the palm of your hand along both sides of any crack, or on all edges around a hole in the plaster. If the plaster is firm, proceed with patching. If the plaster feels spongy or *gives* when you push against it, try to assess how wide an area is loose. Again, if the plaster is loose or failing over a large area there are only two solutions: Cover it over with wallboard or paneling, or remove the old plaster and start anew, either with wallboard or with new plaster.

To cover up a badly cracked ceiling, install a new layer of wallboard on top of the old ceiling.

Photo courtesy USG.

inch of plaster, ¼-inch of lath, and at least 1 inch into the ceiling joists. After applying the wallboard, tape and finish the wallboard joints and corners according to regular taping procedure. To be sure that all joints are full and flat, apply the tape to reinforce the joint, let it dry, apply a first trowel coat and let it dry, and then apply a finish coat. To smooth, sand with a wet sponge or wallboard wet-sander.

If a ceiling is sagging badly or the plaster is buckled, you must apply 1″ × 2″ furring strips over plaster, perpendicular (at right angles) to the old joists. Use a carpenter's level and cedar shims (available at home centers) to shim and level the furring strips, then apply wallboard as above. Furring and leveling a ceiling can be a bit complicated, and you might want to hire a professional for this job.

Note that covering over the old plaster ceilings, either with wallboard or with fur-

ring strips and wallboard, as opposed to first removing the old plaster is recommended. These approaches avoid the work, mess and disposal problems associated with plaster removal. But be aware that failed plaster walls present a different set of problems. Adding a layer of wallboard over existing plaster walls is more difficult than over ceilings because the trim interferes with wallboard placement. You must either remove all the trim and shim out the window and doorframes (with wood strips) to match the thickness of the added wallboard, or you must install wood or metal edge moldings on the new wallboard to conceal the joint where wallboard and trim meet. Because of this extra work, and because of current concerns for energy conservation, many people elect to remove damaged plaster from walls, add insulation and a vapor barrier to the exterior walls, then apply new walls of wallboard.

Wallboard

Wallboard has largely replaced plaster in residential construction as a covering material for interior walls. Wallboard will *give*, or flex slightly, as the framing settles, so cracks in wallboard are rare compared to the number of cracks in more-brittle plaster. When they do occur in wallboard construction, cracks generally show up at corners and at header joints above doors or windows. Both of these areas are areas of maximum stress from settling and shrinking of framing lumber. If cracks in wallboard construction are wide or numerous, have an engineer inspect the building and assess whether the footings or foundations are failing.

Repairing Cracks in Wallboard

To repair minor cracks in wallboard, tape them as you would tape joints in new wallboard construction. This calls for a first coat of reinforcing tape, a leveling coat, a second trowel coat and sanding. Be sure to allow a proper drying interval between each coat of taping compound. This is nec-

Scrape away loose paper or plaster from the crack.

Use the taping knife to apply a thin coat of taping compound over the crack. Center and embed the wallboard tape in the compound.

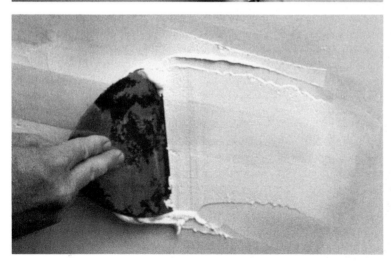

essary to be sure that the compound has undergone maximum shrinkage after each coat.

Hanging Pictures on Wallboard

Whether you are installing a smoke alarm, a small fixture, or hanging a picture or mirror, fastening any product to a hollow wallboard wall can be a problem. The answer to the problem is to check out the many anchor systems available at your hardware dealer. The options include metal Molly bolts or plastic anchors that collapse/expand when a screw is driven into them.

An example of these hollow wall anchors is the Rawlplug Zip-It. The fastener system consists of a DuPont Zytel nylon anchor that drills its own hole as it is driven into wallboard with a Phillips screwdriver. When the threaded plastic anchor is

Use the taping knife to wipe excess compound from under the tape. Immediately apply compound in a thin coat over the tape and let dry. When tape is dry apply another thin coat of compound to smooth and conceal the tape.

seated, a sheet metal screw is driven into the anchor; the anchor expands to grip the edges of the wallboard hole. Removal of the anchor is accomplished by simply reversing the direction of the screwdriver to extract the screw and anchor.

Fastener Failures

Fastener failure was once referred to as *nail pops*, but for years wallboard has been installed with wallboard (drywall) screws, so the current reference is to fastener failures. These popped fastener heads, whether occurring with nails or with screws, are the result either of using fasteners that are too long, or of applying the wallboard panels over framing lumber that has a high moisture content. As wet lumber dries out it undergoes excessive shrinkage, and this excess shrinkage causes the fastener head to protrude or *pop* above the wallboard surface. This phenomenon can also be seen in popped nails in exterior siding, or in popped nails in the underlayment under vinyl or linoleum sheet floorcovering. Because they occur on interior finished walls, fastener failures are most objectionable in wallboard on walls and ceilings.

To prevent fastener failures in remodeling jobs, always use kiln-dried framing lumber, and always use the right length of nails or screws for fastening materials. The pop (or exposure of the fastener head) will be directly proportional to the depth to which the fastener penetrates the framing lumber. To clarify, if a fastener is so long that it penetrates one-half of the stud width, or 1¾ inches (one-half of 3½ inches) the degree of pop on the head will be equal to the shrinkage in that thickness of lumber. But if a proper fastener length is observed, using 1¼-inch-long ring shank wallboard nails or 1-inch-long wallboard screws, the depth of wood penetration is minimized to only ½- to ¾-inch of wood. The amount of shrinkage in so little wood will be minimal, as will the pop on the head of the fastener.

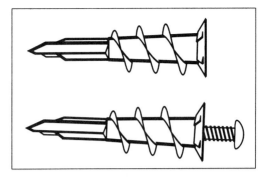

The two-piece Zip-It anchor and screw system.

Courtesy of Rawlplug Co. Inc.

Use a Phillips screwdriver to drive the Zip-It anchor into the wallboard.

Courtesy of Rawlplug Co. Inc.

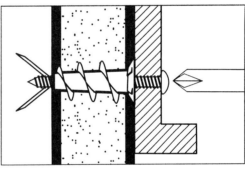

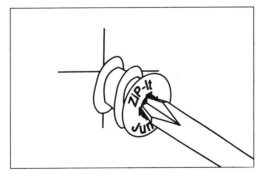

When the anchor is driven flush with the wall surface, drive in a screw to secure a mirror, shelf bracket or other object.

Courtesy of Rawlplug Co. Inc.

To repair fastener failures or pops in wallboard, use a wallboard screw gun to drive new screws within 2 inches of the popped fastener. Then use a hammer to drive the popped fastener so the head is dimpled below the surface of the wallboard. Do this to all popped fasteners. Then apply three coats of wallboard taping compound over both the new screw head

Use wallboard screws rather than nails to eliminate fastener failures, or pops, and to securely fasten loose wallboard.

Photo courtesy of Sears.

and the dimpled head of the popped fastener, allowing drying time between coats. To smooth, wet-sand with a sponge or wallboard wet-sander. Then apply a coat of primer over the entire wall or ceiling and repaint as desired.

Patching Holes in Wallboard

Now that peel-and-stick patches are available, holes in wallboard are easier to repair. These patches consist of a fiber glass backing (with adhesive), and a metal foil center for patch rigidity. For repairing holes up to 6 inches in diameter, just peel the covering off the adhesive backing, position the patch so it is centered over the hole, and cover the patch with two thin coats of taping compound to smooth it. Allow drying time between the two coats of compound and smooth with a wet sponge or a wallboard wet-sander.

Preparing Wallboard for Paint

We offer interior painting advice in chapter one, "Painting." But be aware that redecorating time is a good time to assess the condition of interior walls or ceilings. (Note: It is difficult to repair ceilings that have been spray textured. The texture must be sanded or removed, the repairs completed, then the area retextured.)

It is easy to spot defects such as hollow or popped nails, ridged joints in tape, and crowned or bulging end joints on walls that are to be repainted. To maximize defect visibility on a wall or ceiling surface, turn out the lights and place a lamp with a bare bulb (or an auto trouble light) so it sidelights across the entire surface. Visually inspect the wall or ceiling from several angles; the strong light will highlight the defects.

Using ready-mixed taping compound, apply one or more coats of compound over joints, nail or screw heads, or any other defect. If a sharp ridge is visible down the center of a joint, apply a thin coat of wallboard compound over the ridge and sand smooth. If the joint shows as a bulge, use a wide trowel or taping knife to widen the treated area on both sides of the joint, making the bulge area more gradual, less abrupt. With the electricity turned off, remove the plates covering electrical outlets and use a finger to fill any cracks between the wallboard and the outlet box. This will not only prevent cracks from marring your decorating job, it will also seal the cracks so air cannot infiltrate around the electrical outlets.

Protecting and Repairing Wallcovering

Bathroom or kitchen wallpaper can get water spots from moisture condensation, or can become sticky from exposure to hair spray or grease. Vinyl wallcoverings are usually easy to wash, but trying to remove hair spray and grease residue can ruin your wallcovering. To protect the wallcoverings, apply a coat of a clear, water-based protectant, such as Ultra Clear, to the entire surface. This protectant will leave a flat sheen and will make wallcoverings more washable.

When you hang wallcovering, save any leftovers to make repairs. If an edge comes loose on wallcovering, use a small brush to apply a thin coat of adhesive to the wall, and then press the loose edge gently into the adhesive using a damp sponge.

If a loose spot or blister appears on the wallcovering, buy an adhesive applicator at the paint store. Slit the edge of the blister with a razor knife and use the applicator to inject adhesive behind the loose covering. Then use a damp sponge to smooth the covering down.

If wallcovering is damaged, cut a piece of leftover covering large enough to overlap the damaged area. Be sure you choose a patch with a pattern that matches the damaged area. Hold the patch material over the damaged area, align the pattern on the patch with the pattern on the wall, and use masking tape to secure the patch material in place on top of the damaged spot. Use a razor knife to cut through both the patch and the wallcovering simultaneously. Set the patch aside and wet a sponge. Use the sponge to soak the damaged covering off the wall. Apply wallcovering adhesive to the back of the patch material and carefully fit it into the cutout hole where you removed the damaged covering. Wring out the sponge until it is only damp and wipe the patch so it is tight to the wall and all excess adhesive is removed.

Removing Wallcovering

Removing wallcovering is one job that frequently frustrates DIYers. The reason is that the worker often only wets the surface of the covering, and, seeing that the surface looks wet, assumes it is time to scrape. In removing wallcovering the goal is not just to wet the covering surface, but to get enough moisture under the covering to completely liquify the adhesive. Once the adhesive is softened the covering can be pulled away easily. The key to removing wallcovering is patience.

Modern wallcoverings are strippable, so they are relatively easy to remove. If you

The easy way to repair a hole in wallboard is to use a peel-and-stick patch. The patch is a pregummed fiber glass material with a wire-mesh reinforcement.

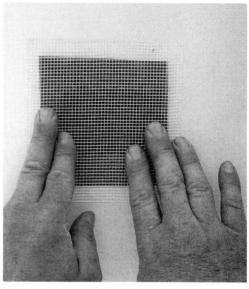

Peel the protective cover off the back of the patch and press the patch in place over the hole.

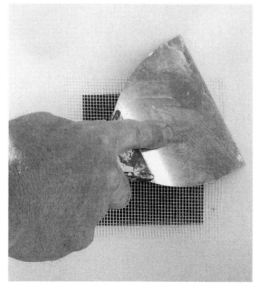

Apply a thin film of wallboard compound over the patch and let it dry, then apply a second coat of compound to smooth and conceal the patch.

Cut a piece of scrap wallcovering with a pattern to match the damaged area and large enough to cover the hole. Tape the patch over the damaged area.

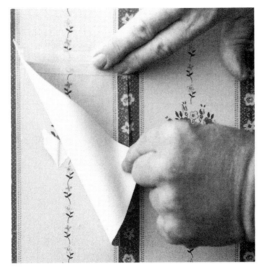

Use a razor knife to cut completely through the patch *and* the existing wallcovering.

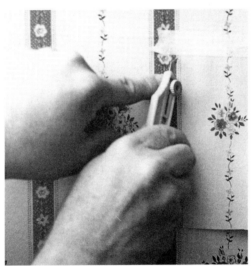

Use a sponge to dampen the wall-covering and carefully remove the damaged covering. The patch will be an exact match both in size and pattern.

want to remove wallcovering, first lift a corner of the covering and pull at it. If the covering pulls free with little effort it is strippable. In some cases the face covering material will strip away but will leave the paper backing on the wall. Simply strip the covering away, then wash the paper backing and adhesive away with a sponge. Wallcovering removal liquid, available at decorating centers, is helpful for dissolving the adhesive.

If the covering does not strip away when you try to remove it, you will have to soak the covering to soften the adhesive. If the covering is vinyl it may be difficult to get moisture to pass through it. You can buy a serrated tool (Paper Tiger is one brand) to slice small slits through the covering to allow the moisture to pass through and reach the adhesive. Then use a sponge or sponge mop to apply hot water and remover liquid to the surface to dissolve the adhesive. After wetting a large area several times, allowing soaking time between each application, test the covering with a scraper. When the adhesive is soft, the covering can be easily removed.

Hot water and a sponge will remove most wallcoverings. If you have a particu-

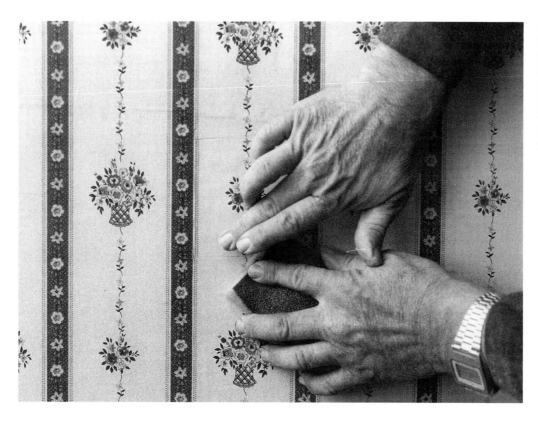

Apply adhesive to the back of the patch and carefully fit the patch into the hole. Use a damp sponge to smooth the patch and to remove excess adhesive.

larly stubborn covering you can rent or buy a wallcovering steamer to help dissolve the adhesive.

Walls and Ceilings Checklist

• Patch holes and cracks in plaster walls.

• Check plaster ceilings for loose, failing areas. You may need to apply ½-inch wallboard over the old plaster.

• Repair minor cracks in wallboard by taping them.

• To prevent fastener failures, use the proper length of nails or screws for fastening wallboard.

• To repair fastener failures, drive screws near the popped fastener, drive the popped fastener below the surface, and cover the repair with taping compound.

• Save leftover wallcovering to make repairs.

• Check to see if wallcovering to be removed is strippable. If not, soak the covering to thoroughly soften the adhesive for removal.

The secret to painless wallcovering removal is to soak the covering until the adhesive is softened. Most wallcovering can be removed using a sponge and hot water. Use a steamer to remove stubborn coverings.

Photo courtesy Black & Decker.

FLOORS AND STAIRS

Cleaning Hardwood Floors

To clean away grit and dirt, first vacuum the hardwood floor. If the floor has a heavy wax buildup, use odorless mineral spirits or a packaged floor cleaner product (available at paint stores) to strip the old wax away. After cleaning, rub down the floor using a clean dry cloth or fine (0000) steel wool. When the floor is clean and dry, buff the finish with a rented buffing machine. Apply a cleaner/paste wax or a straight paste wax to protect the finish. **Note:** The hardwood flooring industry for years has recommended that any hardwood floor, even prefinished hardwood, be protected with a coat of paste wax. However, if wax has been used on the floor, flooring contractors have reported difficulty in refinishing floors with a polyurethane finish. The problem is that when refinishing, the new coat of polyurethane will not adhere properly to any wax residue on the flooring. These contractors now recommend that hardwood flooring with a polyurethane finish not be waxed, and that, beyond cleaning, future flooring maintenance be limited to sanding and recoating with polyurethane. If you are buying new prefinished flooring, or having older floors sanded and refinished, ask the dealer or contractor to advise you regarding maintenance instructions for your particular finish.

Stains on Hardwood

Most hardwoods will stain (turn black) when exposed to moisture. This is commonly seen on window frames or trim, where condensation from the windowpanes runs down and stains the wood, but hardwood floors will also turn black if subjected to moisture. This staining may be caused by spilled water—from watering houseplants, for example—but a more common cause is from pet urine. Moisture on finished wood first peels away the varnish or polyurethane finish and then activates the tannin in the wood, causing the black or dark brown stains.

First, a precaution: As with any home repair, be very careful to limit repair efforts to only the damaged area. Extending the repair over a much wider area simply means that the repair will be more visible on the finished floor. To remove stains from hardwood floors or trim, sand away the peeled or cracked finish. After sanding, apply a wood bleach, such as oxalic acid, to the stained area. Oxalic acid is available in crystal form, to be mixed with water, from most paint stores. If the stain is very dark, soak a clean cotton cloth or piece of white toweling in the oxalic acid. Cover the stain and leave the cloth in place until the wood is bleached to match the surrounding wood. When the stain is gone, rinse the wood with vinegar and let the repair area dry.

When the area is dry, apply a coat of wood restorer to the bleached area. A variety of wood cleaners and restorers is available at paint stores. To restore the bleached wood to the same color as the existing floor, several coats of wood restorer may be needed.

Sanding Hardwood Floors

When considering whether to sand hardwood floors or not, my advice would be: *Don't do it.* In many or most cases, hardwood flooring can be repaired, stripped and refinished without resorting to floor sanding. When sanding a floor to remove scratch marks, gouges or existing finishes, one must remove some portion of the wood stock, reducing both the thickness and the stiffness of the wood flooring. If too much stock is removed the flooring can become flexible when walked on, and this flexibility can contribute to annoying floor squeaks.

Have an experienced floor sanding contractor assess the condition of the flooring and suggest the right refinishing steps. Modern latex wood patchers can be used to fill scratches or gouges in the hardwood floor, and stripping the floor can permit refinishing without sanding.

There is a real art to running a floor-sanding machine. One must move the sander over the floor with a measured rhythm and speed to avoid uneven sanding (wood removal). The sander must always be run *with* the grain to achieve a scratch-free finish. If the contractor insists that sanding the flooring is the right course, get several bids from sanding contractors and have the work professionally done. To find a reliable contractor, look in the Yellow Pages under "Floor Laying, Refinishing and Resurfacing."

Correcting an Uneven Hardwood Floor

Hardwood floors sometimes warp or buckle, presenting a problem. The cause of this warpage may be too much humidity in the house, inadequate or uneven nailing by the floorlayer, or failure to leave expansion space around the perimeter of the floor so the hardwood has room to expand and contract as temperatures and humidity change. If a hardwood floor appears to be warped, buckled or uneven it may still be worth saving. As noted above, sanding away too much stock may leave the floor strips too thin, so they flex and squeak when they are walked on. If the floor is very uneven the remedy may be to pull up the floor and re-lay it. This is a somewhat tough task, because you must remove the flooring strips carefully, working on your knees with a prybar. You must work slowly, because the hardwood strips become dry and brittle with age and will crack easily if they are forced.

Taking Up the Old Floor

To take up and re-lay a hardwood floor, first remove the base molding and shoe. Use a thin prybar for this task, prying only at nail locations to avoid splitting the trim. Set the base trim aside for future replacement.

With the base trim removed, begin to pry up the flooring strips. The narrow wood strips are tongue-and-groove, and most hardwood floors must be removed starting with the last row first. In most rooms the floorlayer started at the outside wall, nailing in the first row of flooring with the tongue side toward the inside of the house. Then the next row of strips was laid with the groove of each strip fit over the tongue of the preceding strip, with the tongue of the strip again on the inside of the room. This means that you must remove the flooring strips in reverse order: That is, start removing the flooring strips by prying up the strip along the inside wall, then proceeding across the room, removing the strips outward to the exterior wall.

To re-lay the floor you must keep track of the flooring strips as you remove them, so you can re-lay them in the same order. If possible lay out the flooring strips on a basement or garage floor, just as you took them up, so they are in order for re-laying.

As you remove the flooring strips you must remove the nails from them. The best way to do this is to use pliers and pull the nail *through* the flooring strip from the back. If you try to drive the old flooring nails out through the face with a hammer you may splinter or crack the wood.

You may also have to clean the flooring strips to remove residue such as floor filler, varnish or wax. Clean the strips carefully, using a piece of sandpaper and a sharp chisel to clean the edges.

When you have taken up all the old flooring, check the subfloor. Renail any loose subfloor boards. Then lay flooring paper down over the subfloor, overlapping the paper seams by at least 2 inches. Some carpenters today eliminate the use of flooring paper between floor and subfloor. The flooring paper provides a cushion between the subfloor and hardwood floor, however, so I recommend using it as extra insurance against future squeaks.

Re-laying the Floor

When you lay the first strip of flooring leave at least ½-inch gap between the strip and the wall or sole plate. This provides room for the flooring to expand. Lay the first row of strips with the tongue side facing into the room, driving nails down through the face of the strips. Then lay the second row. Dry and brittle flooring will crack if you try to nail directly through it. Predrill a hole through the tongue of the flooring strip at a 45-degree angle, placing a flooring nail at each floor joist location. Using a carpenter's finish hammer, drive flooring nails into each joist, and set the nail head with a nail set. Nailing through the tongue of the board lets you *blind nail*, i.e., drive the nails in such a way that the heads are concealed. Proceed across the floor until you have reached the inside wall.

At the inside wall, again do not force the flooring boards tight against the wall or the sole plate. Leave at least ½-inch gap so the floor can expand. Remember that the base trim will cover the crack at the edge of the floor. Because you cannot angle a flooring nail so close to the wall, you will have to *face-nail* the last three or four strips of flooring. Face-nailing means that you will have to drive the nails straight down through the face of the flooring, rather than angling the nails through the tongue as you did on the other flooring strips.

When the floor is totally re-laid it must be sanded and refinished. Unless you have some sanding experience I recommend that you have the floor sanded by a pro. My experience has proven that sanding floors is one of those jobs that is difficult for an amateur to do well.

Silencing Floor Squeaks

One of the most common homeowner complaints is squeaking floors. Hardwood floors consist of: floor joists, subflooring (usually 1″ × 6″ planks or ¾-inch plywood), and a layer of rosin or tar paper, with the finished hardwood floor on top. Usually, the floorlayer installs red-rosin paper between the subfloor and the underlayment or finished flooring. But if the rosin paper is omitted, the joists settle or nails become loose, the various components may rub against one another and cause the floor to squeak.

Floor joists that are not large enough for their span can flex and sag under a person's weight, and this can cause squeaking floors. Too-small floor joists are a common problem in older houses, but modern building codes and inspection schedules have all but eliminated the problem in the past few decades.

Plumbing pipes are often secured to the bottom of the floor joists via V-shaped metal pipe hangers. These pipes can rub against the bottom edge of the floor joists when someone walks across the floor and the floor joists flex under that weight. Sheet metal furnace ducts, like water or drain pipes, can also make a noise when they flex due to weight from above. Also, metal or wooden bridging may be positioned in an *X* shape between floor joists. This bridging can squeak if one piece rubs against another.

If the basement side of the floor is unfinished and accessible, you can stop most floor squeaks. If the bottom side of the floor joists are covered—i.e., if the ceiling of the basement is finished and floor joists are not accessible—squeaks will be difficult to cure without removing the basement ceiling covering.

To determine the source of your floor squeak, stand in the basement or a first-floor room and have a helper walk across the floor above you. Note the spots where squeaks occur, and have your helper step repeatedly on those spots until you have pinpointed the source. If there are multiple squeaks over an entire floor, carry a piece of chalk and mark the floor joists where squeaks occur.

If the squeak is the result of bridging rubbing together, use a prybar to separate the bridging slightly so the members do not rub against each other. If the noise is coming from plumbing pipes, use a hammer to pull away the metal joist hangers and reset them so the pipe is held loosely against the bottom of the floor joists.

If the squeaks are caused by layers of subflooring, underlayment and/or finished flooring rubbing against each other, and the floor is open from the underside, use a wallboard screw gun and wallboard screws to screw the flooring layers together and stop any intrafloor squeaks. Be sure the wallboard screws are short enough so they do not go completely through the finish layer of flooring.

If the floors are not accessible from the underside, as would be true of second-story floors with finished ceilings below, you must face-nail the flooring to quiet squeaks. If you have carpet covering the floors, carpet replacement time is the best time to surface-nail the flooring. To surface-nail flooring you simply predrill small holes through the finish flooring, drive ring-shank or annular flooring nails to lock the subfloor and underlayment (or finish flooring) together so they can't move against one another and create the squeaking noise. Nails driven through the surface of finish flooring should be driven below the floor surface with a nail set, then puttied to conceal the nail holes.

Leveling a Sagging Floor

If floor joists sag, bounce or are "springy" when walked upon, you can double the floor joists to stiffen them. Select new floor joists the same size as the existing joists (for example, $2' \times 10' \times 12'$ long). Position a new joist alongside the existing joist, with one end of the joist resting on the basement wall or foundation and the opposite end resting on the center bearing wall or steel I-beam. If the existing beam is sagging, jack it up until it's level. Spike the new floor joist to the existing joist using 8d nails. Double all the floor joists the same way so that the joists are now spiked together in pairs. Note that you will have to remove any floor bridging before installing the new floor joists.

To level a sagging floor place a 2″ × 4″ atop a hydraulic jack and jack the sagging joist up until it is level. Then position a second floor joist against the sagging joist, with the ends resting on the foundation or support beam.

Use 16d nails or wallboard screws, driven at 16-inch intervals, to fasten the new joist to the sagging joist. Do not remove the supporting jack until the doubled joists are fastened together.

Repairing Squeaking Stairs

If steps on stairs squeak, the problem is usually caused by the tread (the part you step on) rubbing against the riser (the upright board between the treads). To quiet noisy stairs, secure a supply of (scrap) wood blocks. Apply a generous coating of carpenter's glue to two sides of the scrap block; working from the underside of the stairs, push the two glued surfaces in place in the corners where treads and risers meet. Use small nails to hold the glued blocks in place until the glue sets.

If the stairs have a finish of plaster or wallboard on the underside so that the stairs are not accessible from the bottom, drive flooring nails through the edges of the treads into the risers below. This will lock the treads and risers together so they cannot move and cause squeaks.

Repairing Carpet

If carpet is not properly stretched when it is laid it will soon develop wrinkles. Carpet wrinkles not only look unsightly but the feet tend to drag across the peaks of the wrinkles and cause premature carpet wear. The solution is to have the carpet restretched to remove the wrinkles and smooth the carpet. Restretching carpet is a job for a pro.

If your carpet has a hole or stain that is less than 3½ inches in diameter you can repair it yourself. You must have a small piece of scrap carpet to make the repair (cut one from inside a closet or underneath a large piece of furniture, if necessary).

From a carpet store buy a circular tool called a *cookie cutter*. The cookie cutter has two razor blades that cut through the carpet as you turn the tool. Also buy an adhesive bandage to be positioned in the hole in the carpet to hold the patch in place.

Position the cookie cutter over the damaged area. Push downward with gentle pressure as you turn the tool. Increase the pressure as you turn the tool through several revolutions until you have cut completely through the carpet. Now use the tool the same way to cut a circular patch from the carpet scrap.

Peel the backing from the adhesive bandage and position the bandage in the carpet hole. The bandage is oversized so that it will overlap the hole and grip the carpet backing. When the adhesive bandage is in place, insert the patch into the hole and press it firmly in place against the adhesive bandage. Use the edge of a quarter, a comb or a vacuum cleaner to fluff and blend the carpet fibers around the edge of the hole.

Floors and Stairs Checklist

- Apply wood bleach only to stained area to remove stains from hardwood floors. After drying, apply wood restorer.
- Leave sanding hardwood floors to the pros.
- To correct an uneven hardwood floor, remove flooring strips carefully, starting with the last row. Keep track of flooring strips so you can re-lay them in the same order. Renail any loose subflooring. Leave room for the flooring to expand (½ inch between first strip and wall). Sand and refinish.
- Shim flooring and floor joists from the basement to fix squeaky hardwood floors caused by floor joists rubbing against plumbing pipes or by bridging pieces rubbing together.

Use a circular tool called a *cookie cutter* to remove the damaged area of carpet.

Cut a replacement carpet disk from a scrap piece of carpet. Peel the backing from the carpet bandage and place the bandage in the hole, sticky side up.

Place the carpet patch in the hole and press it firmly in place against the adhesive bandage. Use a comb or vacuum cleaner to raise the carpet nap and help conceal the patch.

- Correct sagging floor joists by spiking a new floor joist to the old one, jacking it level.
- Glue wood blocks in the corners underneath to quiet noisy stairs.
- Repair small holes or stains in carpet with a cookie cutter, scrap carpet and adhesive carpet bandage.

WINDOWS AND DOORS
Weatherstripping a Window
In the average house, windows account for about 17 percent of energy loss. Replacing the existing windows with new, energy-efficient models is expensive, and may require many years to get a payback (i.e., save enough energy cost to pay for the new windows). Keep in mind that in addition to actual energy dollar savings, new windows can reduce drafts and make the family more comfortable, and can also enhance the appearance, or curb appeal, of the house.

If windows are leaking air, you must replace the old weatherstripping. Easy-to-install adhesive-backed weatherstrips are available. Just remove the covering strips from the adhesive backing and press the new strips firmly in place along the window cracks.

For a more permanent solution to leaking windows, you can replace the primary weatherstripping. Window repair kits include new window guides, weatherstrips and nails. To install new primary weatherstripping you must first remove the window stops at the front of the window sash. The stops are the wood strips that hold the window sash in the channel. Pry these away carefully so as not to break the stops. (You'll need to replace the stops after installing new weatherstripping.) After removing the window stops, pull the window sash forward and unhook the springs or sash cords from the sash. You can now remove the window sash from the opening. Use a small prybar to pry out the brads holding the old window guides and weatherstripping in place. Install new guides and weatherstripping, then replace the window

sash in the frame. Nail or screw the window stops in place.

Curing a Sticking Window
When painting windows you should avoid letting paint run or drip into the cracks between the window sashes and the stops that hold the windows in place. Paint that runs into the cracks and dries there will bond the sash and stops together, and you will not be able to open the window after the paint dries. To minimize sticking windows, work with a "dry" paintbrush so there is little excess paint to run into cracks in the window frame. Also, while painting the windows or waiting for the painted windows to dry, move the sash up and down frequently to avoid having windows that are painted shut.

If you have windows that are difficult or impossible to open, a paint buildup between the sash and window stop may be the culprit. Do not try to force the window open: You may damage the window. Instead, buy a small tool called a *paint zipper*. The paint zipper has a wooden handle and a triangular-shaped, serrated (toothed) head. To cut the paint film between the window sash and stops, push the paint zipper into the cracks around the sash and use a sawing motion to cut the paint film and free the window in its tracks. Now try the window: If it doesn't move, work the paint zipper around the window cracks again. You will free the window so it will open without being forced.

When you have opened the window, sand away any ridges or paint buildup from the window sash. Use a vacuum cleaner to clean grit and dirt from the window tracks. Lubricate the tracks lightly with WD-40 so the windows will move freely.

Weatherstripping a Door
New entry doors may have a magnetic weatherstrip similar to the door on a refrigerator. Older doors often have the brass V-weatherstrip, a metallic strip that has the point of the V facing inward. As the door

To free a sticking window, use a serrated tool called a *paint zipper* to cut the paint film between the window stop and sash. Do not force the window. Repeated cuts with the zipper may be necessary to cut through a stubborn paint sag.

is closed the legs of the V compress, forming a seal against the door to keep out dirt and air. Check the fit of the V-shaped weatherstrip to be sure it still springs outward against the door. You can use a screwdriver to bend the top leg of the V outward so it will seal more tightly against the door edge.

Perhaps the most important — and the most often overlooked — weatherstrip is the door sweep at the bottom of entry doors. The door sweep is a weatherstrip that seals the crack between the bottom of the door and the threshold. The door sweep prevents air infiltration and also seals the crack so dirt and insects cannot enter.

Check your present door sweep to be sure it fits tightly against the threshold. If the door has no sweep, or if the sweep is more than five years old, check out the new door sweeps now available at home centers. New energy-efficient door sweeps have several layers of vinyl that overlap at the threshold to provide a superior weather seal.

New door sweeps are easy to install. Most sweeps include screws to use with the sweeps. Simply unscrew the old sweep and cut the new sweep (with tin snips or a hacksaw) to the right length, if necessary. Use the new screws to attach the new sweep, driving the new screws into the old screw holes. You can also buy one of the newer adhesive-backed sweeps. To install one of these, first remove the screws holding the old unit in place. Then check the new sweep for length and trim it if necessary. Pull the adhesive backing cover strip away and press the new sweep into position.

Sticking Doors

If an exterior door is sticking, first check the hinges to be sure all the screws are in place and the hinges are tight. Check how the door swings, and use a spray lubricant such as WD-40 to oil the hinges. Exterior

To free up a sticking entry lock, disassemble the lock for cleaning and lubrication as shown. The entire lock assembly is held together with two bolts and two screws.

Maintaining Door Locks

One of life's little frustrations is to come home, night after night, and fumble with a key in a sticking lock. On the firm idea that it is best to eliminate as many frustrations as one possibly can from life, my advice is to take an hour or two to remove, clean and lubricate all door locks.

Most entry and security locks are held in place by two connecting screws. Remove these two screws to remove the inside and outside cylinders or handles. Then remove two screws from the latch bolt faceplate (on the edge of the door, where the latch bolt extends from the door lock). This will permit you to remove the faceplate and the latch bolt shaft. Use an aerosol lubricant such as WD-40 to clean and lubricate the lock mechanism. Reassemble the lock and test it. **Note:** WD-40 dries to a "dry" or non-oily film.

Installing a Deadbolt Lock

The idea that locks are useful for keeping out honest people is reinforced by the ease with which burglars can kick in an ordinary door. Most exterior doors are fitted with ordinary entry locks, and the bolts on these locks ordinarily extend only a short way into the door jamb. A booted foot or a pipe wrench is all that is needed to defeat this type of lock. To increase home security and make entry much more difficult, install a deadbolt lock.

Deadbolt locks have several advantages over ordinary entry door locks. First, deadbolt locks have no exterior knobs, so they cannot be forced with a pipe wrench. Second, the bolt on a deadbolt lock is long enough to extend all the way through the door jamb, meaning that intruders must exert much more force to break in a deadbolt lock.

Deadbolt locks are available in a variety of styles. On some locks you must use a key to open the lock either from the inside or the outside. Other models have a knob for opening the lock from the inside, so occupants can exit without using a key in

doors often have bare, unsealed wood on the edges or ends of the door. This unsealed wood permits moisture to enter. A door that swings freely normally may swell and stick during humid weather. It is a mistake to plane or sand the door during humid weather, because the door will shrink to its original size when dry, hot weather returns, and then the door will be loose in its frame.

If a door is sticking, close and open the door several times, checking the cracks carefully to see at what points the door is sticking. Then fold a piece of fine sandpaper and insert it alongside the doorstop and close the door. If you close/open the door several times, the scrubbing action of the sandpaper will remove a bit of the paint film or door stock and you will be able to open and close the door.

Do not remove more wood from the door: Wait until hot, dry weather returns and see how the door fits then. You can avoid future swelling of the door by applying a coat of clear sealer or a thin film of paint to all the edges and ends of the door so moisture cannot enter.

case of an emergency. Deadbolt locks can be bought for around $15 to $20. Manufacturers also offer a paired set of locks including a deadbolt lock and an entry lock. The advantage of buying the pair is that both locks can be opened with the same key. Be aware, however, that it is not necessary to buy new locks in order to use a single key. Any locksmith can rekey your existing lock to match any new deadbolt lock you install.

To install a deadbolt lock you will need a hole saw. Any hole saw will work to install a lock in a wooden door, but modern steel-clad doors require the use of a hole saw that can cut sheet metal. The common hole saw needed is 2⅛-inch; the lock instructions will tell you what size hole saw to use. You will also need a drill bit, usually either 1-inch or ⅞-inch diameter, to drill the holes for the bolt through the door edge and the frame.

The height for the lock on the door is between 40 and 44 inches from the floor. Measure this height and check to be sure the deadbolt lock will not interfere with the latch or lock on your storm door.

The instructions for installing the deadbolt lock will usually include a paper template. This template can be taped to the door as a guide for drilling the lock hole (with the hole saw) and the bolt hole (with the drill bit).

Using the hole saw, drill through the door first. Watch for the pilot bit of the hole saw to pop through the opposite side of the door, then pull out the hole saw and finish drilling the hole from the other side. This will prevent the hole saw from making a splintered exit hole.

When the lock hole is finished, bore the hole for the bolt on the edge of the door. Then mark and drill a hole through the doorframe. Assemble the lock and install the strike plate on the doorframe. Check frequently as you drill and assemble the lock to be sure that the lock bolt will fit into the bolt hole.

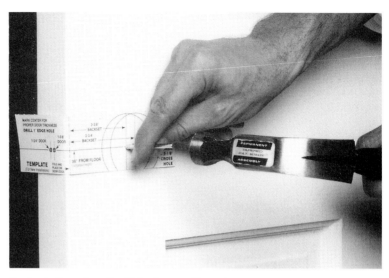

To install a deadbolt lock, position the lock template at the desired location, usually about 44 inches above the door bottom. Secure the template with cellophane tape and use a punch to mark the hole positions for both the lock and the bolt.

Photo courtesy of Stanley Tools.

Windows and Doors Checklist

• Add weatherstripping to windows to improve thermal values.

• Use a paint zipper to cut paint film causing windows to stick.

• Add an energy-efficient door sweep to exterior doors.

• Lubricate hinges of sticking doors, or sand off just enough for the door to open and close easily.

• Install deadbolt locks on all exterior doors.

Drill a pilot hole for the lock bolt in the edge of the door.

Photo courtesy of Stanley Tools.

Use a hole saw to drill a hole for the lock mechanism. To avoid splintering the door, drill through one side until the pilot bit exits on the opposite side. Then remove the hole saw from the first side and finish drilling from the back side.

Photo courtesy of Stanley Tools.

To mark the lock bolt hole on the doorframe, drive a 16d finish nail as shown, from the lock hole through the lock bolt pilot hole. When you have marked the bolt location on the frame use a 1-inch bit to drill the bolt hole in both the door edge and the frame. Assemble the lock in the hole following the instructions included with the lock.

Photo courtesy Stanley Tools.

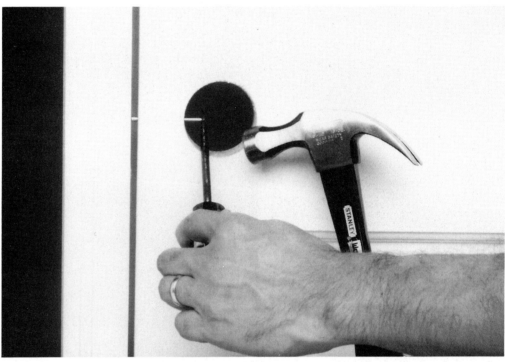

APPLIANCES

Maintaining a Refrigerator

Home refrigerators use an estimated 5 percent of the nation's electricity output. To reduce operating costs and to keep your refrigerator in good working condition, follow these tips:

Check the gasket(s) around the refrigerator and/or freezer compartments. Visually inspect the gaskets to see if they are stiff or cracked: Insert a dollar bill in the door, and close the door, then try to pull the dollar past the gasket. If the bill slips easily out of the door, replace the door gasket. Buy the gasket needed for your make and model of refrigerator. To replace the old gasket, bend the gasket back so you can see the gasket retaining strip. Use a Phillips screwdriver to loosen the screws holding the retaining strip in place. If your refrigerator is a newer model you can now pull the old gasket free. On older models the screws may pass through the holes in the gasket, and you will have to remove the screws completely from the top and about halfway down the sides of the gasket. Then remove the old gasket and fit the new gasket in place. Replace or tighten the retaining strip screws.

Use a cordless hand vacuum, a special brush (about $5 at your appliance dealer) or a clean paintbrush to clean the condensor coil at the back or bottom of the appliance. Do this twice a year and you'll save an estimated $25 in electrical costs annually.

There is a defrost pan or condensate tray at the bottom of your refrigerator. The defrost pan catches water from defrosting, and the water evaporates into the air. However, if the pan is not kept clean, fungus or mold may grow in the pan and can cause bronchial or lung irritation. To clean the defrost pan, remove the cover below the refrigerator door and pull the pan out. Wash the pan: Chlorine bleach will kill spores of mold or mildew. Rinse the pan and wipe it dry.

When it's time to replace your refrigerator, buy an energy-efficient one. According to industry estimates, the cost for electricity to run the appliance for fifteen to twenty years may be triple the cost of the appliance.

Cleaning Electric Stove Surface Elements

After each use, wipe the surface units with soapy water and a soft cloth. Use a soapy scouring pad to remove baked-on food.

Let surface units cool, apply a thin coat of salt-free oil to the surface, and heat for five minutes. Or, ask your appliance dealer to suggest an optional dressing rather than using the oil.

Use a metal cleaner (or a polishing cream for cook tops) to remove any yellowing from stainless-steel rings.

Cleaning a Humidifier

To be sure the water in your humidifier is clean, you should service the humidifier frequently. If you neglect cleaning, micro-organisms can grow in the humidifier tank and become airborne, causing respiratory problems. The Consumer Product Safety Commission (CPSC) suggests that portable humidifiers with less than five-gallon capacity should be cleaned daily and sanitized once a week. Humidifiers of greater capacity (over five gallons) should be sanitized every two weeks.

To clean a humidifier, empty out the water, use a towel to dry the inside of the tank, then refill the tank with clean water. To kill any microorganisms in the humidifier tank, fill the humidifier with a chlorine bleach solution (one part bleach to nine parts water) and let the solution stand in the tank for twenty to thirty minutes. Then rinse the tank with clear water until you can no longer smell the bleach and refill the humidifier.

For furnace-mounted humidifiers, follow the manufacturer's directions for cleaning the unit. Visually inspect the humidifier for signs of mineral or other buildup, and clean as often as conditions indicate.

Maintaining a Garbage Disposal

Save the warranty and maintenance information, and follow the manufacturer's directions for use and maintenance of your disposal unit. You can dispose of most vegetable or food wastes in the disposal unit, but do not insert paper or other packaging, aluminum foil, large bones, cloth tea bags, or any glass or crockery. All disposals are designed to be operated with water flowing while the unit is running. To reduce clogs, the water flushes food particles through the small drainpipe under your sink and into the larger main drain. The water also solidifies any grease or fats so they can be flushed away and will not clog the drain.

If the disposal jams, immediately shut off the power to the unit and remove the splash guard to try to spot the cause of the jam. If the turntable is jammed because of a bone, bottle cap or piece of silverware, do not try to remove the jam with your bare hand. Use a wooden broom handle to pry on the turntable and free it for rotation.

If you can't free the jam by prying on the impeller, check to see if the disposal has a manual reversing switch, located on the lower housing of the disposal. Try turning the reversing switch to free the jam. If using the reversing switch does not free the jam, check the bottom of the motor housing to find a hexagonal-shaped hole. Use the hex wrench that came with the disposal to rotate the motor shaft back and forth until the jam is free. Then push the overload protection button to see whether the disposal will run free. If you have not succeeded in freeing the jam, call in a professional.

If the disposal drain is plugged, turn off the unit and set a pail under the sink trap. Loosen the trap slowly so the trap contents will fall into the pail. Then clean out the trap to see if that is the source of the plug. If that doesn't cure the problem use a drain auger to reach into the drainpipe and dislodge the plug material.

Water Heater Odors

Water that has a disagreeable odor or taste is the result of various chemicals in the water. These tastes and odors can be magnified when the water is heated. If you have a problem with water quality consult your plumber for advice on how to correct the problem. Suspect the following chemicals if your water has:

- **Bitter taste:** Calcium or magnesium chloride
- **Salty taste:** Sodium chloride
- **Medicine taste:** Sulphates
- **Carbonated water:** Low pH water with high carbon dioxide content
- **Rotten egg smell:** Hydrogen sulphide gas

Most of these odor/taste problems can be cured by filtering the water or by replacing the anode rod in the water heater. Do not remove the anode — it is a sort of sacrificial rod that reduces corrosion elsewhere in the water heater. Let your plumber replace your heater anode with a less active one.

Appliances Checklist

- Clean and maintain refrigerator for more efficient energy consumption.
- Clean humidifier regularly with a bleach solution.
- Correct water heater odors/tastes by filtering water or by replacing the anode rod.

BATHROOMS

Replacing a Toilet Seat

If a toilet seat is broken or damaged, buy a replacement seat at a home center. Seat replacement is an easy job. Use a wrench to remove the nuts from the bolts located under the rim of the toilet bowl on either side of the toilet. Pull off the old seat and replace with the new seat, insert the bolts into the holes in the toilet, and tighten the nuts.

Eliminating Toilet Tank Condensation

In hot weather the toilet tank may sweat with condensation caused by the cold water flowing in after a flush and cooling the tank. Any moisture in the bathroom will condense on the tank exterior, then drip and cause puddles on the floor.

There are several remedies for this problem. One easy cure is to wrap a terry cloth cover around the tank. This will help prevent condensation from forming and will absorb any moisture that does form. An optional solution is to install a styrofoam insulation kit inside the toilet tank. Buy the insulation kit at hardware or home-center stores.

Installing a Mixer Valve

When cold water runs into the toilet tank it may cause condensation on the tank. To prevent this condensation replace the water supply valve under the toilet tank with a mixer or three-way valve. This valve mixes hot and cold water to supply the toilet tank with warm water. The toilet tank is thus kept warm so moisture will not condense on the tank's exterior.

Buy a mixer or three-way valve for less than $5 at a plumbing supply store. To install the valve, first shut off the water supply to the toilet. Use a tube cutter to cut the cold and hot water supply pipes. Solder pipe tees into both water lines. Use reduction tees to reduce the water supply pipe size from ½-inch to ⅜-inch diameter. Cut and solder ⅜-inch diameter copper tubing into the tees. Use compression nuts to connect the tubing to the mixer valve. Connect the mixer valve to the water supply tube on the water tank. Turn on the water to test for leaks, then flush the toilet to complete the job check.

Controlling Bathroom Humidity

Because of the high volume of water used in the bathroom — and the fact that water is always standing in the toilet bowl — moisture can become a serious problem in unvented bathrooms. The combination of heat plus moisture can promote mold and mildew growth on tile grout or painted surfaces. Ceramic tile, wallcovering and floorcovering can also become loosened and may result in a costly failure. The resulting mold and mildew can combine to give off an offensive odor.

Installing an Exhaust Fan

To reduce bathroom moisture levels, the first step is to install an exhaust fan. Most exhaust fans come complete with installation instructions. However, fan installation is a rather complicated project, and you may choose to call in a contractor to do the job. You must remove a portion of the plaster or wallboard ceiling, install and wire an electrical control switch, mount the exhaust fan and exhaust duct, and replace and/or repair the area where the ceiling material was removed. The duct must be flashed on the exterior of the house, where it exits through the roof or the wall. If you have all the skills necessary to complete the job, go ahead.

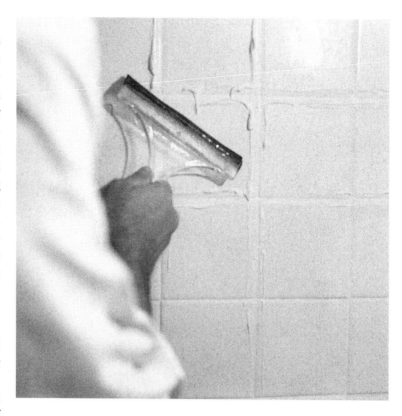

Maintaining Ceramic Tile

To prevent water from entering the joints and loosening the tiles, the joints between ceramic tiles are sealed with grout. It is necessary to inspect ceramic tile joints frequently, because the grout can crack or deteriorate and let water penetrate behind the tiles. Each time you clean the bath check the joints between the tiles, between the tiles and the tub, and between the tub and the floor to be sure all cracks are sealed. If you see an opening or crack in any of the joint materials, you should grout or caulk the crack immediately to prevent water entry behind the tile.

To avoid the mess of mixing, buy ready-mixed latex grout products for grouting ceramic tile. To apply the grout, first clean the tile thoroughly. Use a tile knife to clean the cracked grout from between tiles. Also clean the joint where the tub and tile meet.

Use a rubber squeegee or a sponge to apply the grout over the entire tile surface. Apply grout to all tile-to-tile joints, then use a rubber squeegee to wipe away the excess grout. When you have finished

Use your forefinger to spread latex grout in tile joints; use a window squeegee to remove excess grout.

Use peel-and-stick tub-and-tile caulk to seal the crack between the tile and the bathtub.

applying and wiping down the grout, let the grout set until it is firm. Then use a clean terry cloth towel to wipe away the haze on the tile surface and to polish the tile. You can substitute a lambswool polishing bonnet, chucked into a power drill, to polish the tile. You may also apply a clear sealer to the grout joints. Grout sealer is especially useful for sealing grout from stains caused by minerals or iron in the water, or for slowing mildew growth on grout.

One of the worst joints for cracking is the tub/tile joint. This joint cracks because the weight of water plus the weight of a person in the tub causes the tub to sag down slightly, cracking away from the wall tile. Use a tub-and-tile acrylic latex or silicone caulk rather than grout to seal this critical joint. Or, use one of the preformed cove products available to cover the tub/tile crack.

Checking Water Temperatures

In houses that are equipped with dishwashers the water heater thermostat is usually set at 140°F (60° C). This setting may result in slightly better results for cleaning dishes, but can be dangerously high for bathwater in households where young children are present. Be aware that 140° water will cause serious (third-degree) burns to a child in as little as three seconds. Turning the water thermostat down to 125° (51° C) can reduce third-degree burns by stretching burn time to a three-minute exposure, giving you more time to remove the child from the hot water before injury results. The obvious way to prevent burns to children is to turn down water heater thermostats so that hot water drawn straight from the heater will not burn a child. Check the owner's manual for your water heater for instructions on adjusting the thermostat.

If you have an older model shower faucet control you may get scalded by hot water each time you are showering and someone in the house flushes a toilet or turns on the faucet. This is because a demand on the cold water at another faucet may reduce the cold water flow to the shower head, disturbing the hot and cold water mix you have selected and leaving only hot water available. To avoid this problem install a new single handle, pressure balance control.

Pressure balance controls react to water pressure changes to maintain a constant temperature at the shower head. These pressure balance units can hold the water temperature steady within a couple of degrees, avoiding the burn you get when someone turns on the cold water at another tap in the house. Unless you are very skilled with plumbing, this installation should be done by a professional plumber.

Refinishing a Bathtub

Over time, minerals or harsh cleaners may etch the finish on porcelain bath fixtures, including tubs and sinks. Replacing a bathtub can be an expensive proposition, because you must destroy the wall and ceramic tile to remove the old tub. However, you can have the tub professionally refinished with an epoxy coating for about 30 percent of the cost of replacement. Professionals tell us the cost for an average refinishing job will range anywhere between $250 and $350.

First, although there are do-it-yourself tub refinishing kits available I don't advise you to refinish the tub yourself. The reason for this is that cleaning the tub is the most important step in getting a new finish coat that will not peel. If you do try the job yourself, you should use a strong solution of TSP (trisodium phosphate) and follow the same steps as the pros. Professional refinishers:

• Wash the tub with an acid/detergent emulsion, rinse and let dry.

• Etch the finish with hydrofluoric acid. **Note:** Acid solutions are very effective but very dangerous for the amateur to handle; DIYers should use *only* concentrated TSP as a cleaner.

• Rinse the cleaner away, wet-sand the tub finish, then rinse and dry. Use automotive type wet-or-dry sandpaper for this job.

• Wipe the tub down with a solvent.

• Apply an undercoat, let it dry, then apply two or three finish coats of epoxy in the color of your choice.

Most amateurs fail at refinishing a bathtub because they do not clean the tub properly. The finish surface of a bathtub will seem smooth to the amateur, but soap residue that remains in the tiny pores of the finish can cause the new coatings to peel.

To find a bathtub refinisher, look in the Yellow Pages under "Bathtubs & Sinks — Repairing & Refinishing." If you live in a small town, check the phone book of a larger city (phone books are available at the public library). Most repair firms will travel the state, setting up appointments in advance. Check out the company you choose with the Better Business Bureau to see if there have been customer complaints, and ask for a list of satisfied customers.

Tub refinishing should last at least eight to twelve years. Beware of those who promise longer finish life, or who claim to be using some sort of synthetic porcelain: There is no such thing. Porcelain is fired at 1,600°F (871°C) and cannot be applied in the home.

Creating a Barrier-Free Bathroom

To make the bathroom barrier-free (that is, accessible to less abled people) be sure the door is wide enough to admit a wheelchair — at least 32 inches wide. Equip the door with a lever-type doorknob, rather than the familiar round knob, as an aid to people who have arthritis or reduced hand strength. Provide grab bars, which are easily installed, alongside the bathtub, at standing/showering height and beside the toilet.

Install brighter lighting for bathroom safety, particularly to avoid dangerous mistakes when taking medication. Remember that an eighty-year-old person may need three times as much illumination for good vision as a twenty-year-old person. Make sure the bathroom floor and the tub/shower are slip resistant.

Bathrooms Checklist

- Install a mixer valve to correct toilet tank condensation.
- Install an exhaust fan to prevent mold and mildew in the bathroom.
- Inspect ceramic tile joints frequently; grout or caulk any cracks immediately.
- Leave bathtub refinishing to the professionals.
- Consider creating a barrier-free bathroom: wide doorway, grab bars, bright lighting, and a slip-resistant floor and tub.

FIREPLACES

Cleaning a Fireplace and Chimney

A common DIY problem is how to clean the brick or stone face, or surround, on a fireplace. TSP (trisodium phosphate) is a powder that can be mixed to any concentration or strength, depending on your cleaning needs. To clean smoke off the fireplace surround use a heavy concentrate of TSP, applied with a stiff scrub brush. Try this on a small area: If the brick or other fireplace facing material does not come clean, call a janitorial supply service and ask them to suggest a commercial cleaner. Look in the Yellow Pages under "Janitorial Equipment and Supplies."

If the chimney is left uncleaned, soot and creosote can build up and can lead to a disastrous chimney fire. You can inspect the chimney yourself by shining a bright light (such as a mechanic's trouble light) up the chimney. If you see a creosote buildup ¼-inch-thick or more it's time to clean the chimney.

Because special tools are needed and the cost of professional service is low, cleaning a fireplace chimney is not a DIY job. Have your fireplace chimney cleaned by a professional chimney sweep. See the Yellow Pages under "Fireplaces" or "Chimney Cleaning." If you have a fire only once a week the chimney should be cleaned every three or four years, but the frequency of cleaning depends on how often you use the fireplace. Let your expert decide on the right cleaning interval.

Repairing a Chimney Cap

Modern fireplace chimneys are built with red clay chimney tile, or liners, surrounded by a veneer of stone or brick. To close the space between the chimney tiles and brick or stone there often is a concrete ring, or cap, atop the chimney. This concrete cap is exposed to water and to freezing temperatures, and often it becomes pitted or cracked. To repair the chimney cap, mix ordinary Portland cement into a heavy paint-like paste and use a nylon brush to spread the cement into the pits and cracks of the chimney cap. This will seal the cap surface and will retard any further weathering and erosion of the concrete cap.

Often the brick veneer on the chimney will crack, or the face of the bricks may pop or spall off. Once the face of the bricks is removed, water will penetrate into the soft brick and will continue to erode it. The only repair for damaged fireplace chimney brick is to remove the brick courses down to the level where bricks are undamaged, then re-lay the courses to replace the damaged bricks. Because of the problems of matching the brick and mortar colors and the degree of expertise needed for this job, I suggest that a professional brick mason be hired to do it. The cost for this repair will vary depending on the geographic area and the type of brick. For price comparison, for one job I checked in a major metropolitan area (Minneapolis/St. Paul, Minnesota) the cost for removing and replacing the top four courses, or brick rows, on a chimney was $500.

Controlling Chimney Pests

To keep squirrels, raccoons, bats or other animal pests out of the fireplace chimney, install a chimney screen atop the chimney. If you already have unwanted guests in the chimney, try using light and noise in the daytime to drive the animals out. In the middle of the day set a powerful light, such as an auto trouble light, so it shines up the chimney. Set a radio in the fire chamber and turn up the volume. Experiments have shown that raccoons are most irritated by talk radio. When the animals have vacated the chimney, install a chimney screen to serve as a permanent barrier to animal pests.

If the combination of light and noise does not get rid of the animals, light a fire at dusk to encourage the nocturnal pests to move outside, then install a chimney screen or a spark arrester to prevent the animals from reentering.

Fireplace Checklist

- Clean the brick or stone surround on a fireplace with trisodium phosphate solution and stiff brush.
- Have chimney cleaned regularly by a professional.
- Seal and protect a cracked chimney cap with a paste of Portland cement.
- Install a chimney screen to keep out pests.

CONSERVING ENERGY

At this writing there are murmurs from the government about passing a new BTU tax. If the plan is adopted it can only lead to higher home utility bills and an increased interest in conservation. To be most effective in reducing home energy use it is important to realize that space heating/air-conditioning is the largest user of energy; water heating is second and appliances are third. For maximum bang for the conservation buck, one must attack the areas of greatest use, so space heating/air-conditioning is the place to concentrate the most effort.

Space Heating

The cost of conditioning air in the home — either heating or cooling — depends on two factors: the thermal efficiency of the walls, ceilings, doors and windows, and the efficiency of the heating/cooling appliances.

It cannot be stressed too strongly that if your house has old and inefficient heating/cooling equipment, nothing you can do to the thermal envelope or house exterior is going to reduce your energy consumption to any great degree. Because it was cheap to waste energy, forced-air furnaces of the past were made *to waste 35 percent of the fuel burned*. That is to say, they were only 65 percent efficient, and more than one-third of your fuel dollars does nothing more than ensure the exhaust of gasses and products of combustion.

If your home has one of these outmoded furnaces, all the attic insulation in the world will not prevent one-third of your fuel (natural gas or oil) from being wasted up the chimney. So, without going into the details of how today's furnaces and air conditioners are built to be more efficient — furnaces now achieve 97 percent efficiency through induced drafts and more efficient burners and heat exchangers — the one single thing you can do to dramatically reduce home energy consumption is to invest in more efficient heating/cooling equipment. (This is also true for appliances such as water heaters and refrigerators.)

Insulating, Weatherstripping and Caulking

The best advice for improving the energy efficiency of the house structure or *thermal envelope* is to attack those areas where the most heat is lost. For example, although the advice is often to blow in more attic insulation first, only 5 percent of heat is lost through the ceilings: Obviously, the savings possible in this area are limited because the loss represents such a small portion of the whole.

In order of percent of loss (and thus opportunity for savings), the energy loss in the house is: 36 percent through cracks in walls, windows and doors; 21 percent through basement walls and floors; 18 percent through frame walls; 17 percent through windows; and only 5 percent through the ceilings.

As shown above, caulking and weatherstripping all cracks in the house will reduce the high 36 percent energy loss. Caulk any crack between two unmoving building ma-

Where heat loss occurs.

Illustration courtesy Dow Chemical Co.

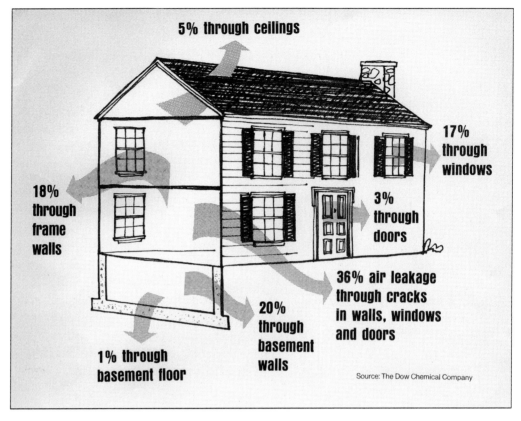

5% through ceilings

17% through windows

18% through frame walls

3% through doors

36% air leakage through cracks in walls, windows and doors

20% through basement walls

1% through basement floor

Source: The Dow Chemical Company

Weatherstripping is easy to apply. Most modern weatherstrips are peel-and-stick or can be installed using brads or screws.

Photo courtesy Black & Decker.

terials: cracks between siding and trim, windows and trim, brick fireplace chimney and siding, or where a water pipe or hose bib penetrates through a hole in the siding.

Apply weatherstripping to any crack between moving materials, such as between the door and frame, or between the window and frame. Weatherstrip all doors, windows and garage doors of attached garages.

Although 21 percent of energy is lost through the basement, only 1 percent of that is lost through the floors: 20 percent is lost through basement walls. This represents an excellent and relatively inexpensive way to conserve energy: insulate basement walls. Just apply furring strips and styrofoam insulation board to the interior surface of concrete basement walls. Use stud adhesive and concrete nails to secure the furring strips to the concrete, and insert styrofoam insulation panels between the furring strips. Or, frame a wood 2″ × 4″ wall against the concrete basement wall and install fiber glass insulation with a plas-

Install door sweeps or base weather-strip using small screws.

tic vapor barrier. Also, cut fiber glass insulation batts to fit in the space above the concrete basement walls, between the concrete and the rim joist, and at the sill plate.

Although 18 percent of energy loss is through frame walls, I have never been an advocate for blowing insulation into wall cavities. If you are remodeling the inside or replacing the siding, by all means install insulation while the stud cavities are open. I have talked to thousands of people and no one claimed high energy savings and satisfaction with having insulation blown through holes and into stud cavities.

Reducing the 17 percent of energy lost through windows can be as easy and inexpensive as having all window weatherstripping replaced, or as expensive as total window replacement. New windows are constructed to be super-tight, with limited air infiltration. In addition, windows have thermal breaks and double glazing to reduce energy loss. Replacing all windows, however, is an expensive project, and payback through saved energy can take years.

Caulk or fill all cracks to reduce air infiltration and drafts.
Photo courtesy of DAP Co.

When caulking, don't overlook exterior wall penetrations such as pipe or wire entries.

Photo courtesy of UGL.

tive new exterior doors can improve the curb appeal and value of your house, reduce painting maintenance (assuming you buy prefinished, super-insulated metal doors), and increase security against any break-ins.

Consider also that direct dollar payback is not the end-all of tightening up the house. Although conservation and budgetary considerations are important, *personal comfort* is also worth considering. For example, caulking cracks not only reduces energy use but also stops drafts that can make one uncomfortable.

Energy Conservation Checklist

- Replace old, inefficient heating system with new, energy-efficient furnace.
- Caulk all cracks between unmoving building materials; apply weatherstripping to cracks between moving materials.
- Insulate basement walls.
- Prevent energy loss through windows by weatherstripping or replacing with new thermal windows.

Only 3 percent of energy loss is through the doors, so it is very difficult to pay for new doors with the minor savings available. Keep in mind, however, that attrac-

To insulate basement walls, build a 2″ × 4″ frame wall and install fiber glass batt insulation between the studs. Staple a plastic vapor barrier over the insulated wall.

Photo courtesy of Owens-Corning Fiberglas.

CHAPTER 3

PLUMBING

A professional plumber must understand a number of principles—from water pressure, to proper slope of drainpipes, to providing adequate ventilation to ensure drainpipes empty quietly and completely. But many plumbing maintenance and repair techniques are well within the abilities of the average homeowner, and because hourly wage rates for plumbers are among the highest in the building industry, plumbing repairs offer the DIYer a chance to save a significant amount of money. Here are some precautionary tips for the do-it-yourself plumber.

To protect pipes and fixtures, maintain good water quality. This is usually no problem in major cities, where water treatment is handled by municipality. If you have well water or live in a small town where municipal water is not softened, however, install a softener and/or water filters as recommended by your plumbing contractor. This will prevent plugging of water supply pipes and protect the fixtures and appliances from stains and mineral buildup.

Buy or rent the right tool for the job at hand. It is almost impossible, for example, to remove a kitchen sink faucet without a specialized tool called a *basin wrench*. Having the right tool for the job gives you the professional advantage.

Do not postpone plumbing maintenance tasks. For example, the homeowner with a leaking faucet will often torque on the faucet handle, trying to force it to shut off. If you push too hard on a faucet you may distort the faucet body, and you will be faced with a faucet replacement instead of a simple repair.

The best protection from emergency plumbing calls and high service bills is good plumbing maintenance.

FIXING LEAKING FAUCETS

The most common plumbing repair may be fixing a leaking faucet. To repair your faucet you must know the manufacturer and the type of faucet you have. Three basic types of faucets are available. They are the compression faucet, the cartridge faucet and the ball-type faucet. Repair procedure for each of these faucets is simple, but you must determine which type you have and be very careful that you obtain the right repair parts for your particular faucet. Repair parts vary not only by faucet type but by manufacturer, so be sure you know the name of the manufacturer before shopping for parts. The manufacturer's name is usually stamped on either the index cap or the faucet body.

When shopping for washers and O-rings to repair a leaking compression faucet, buy an assortment pack or take the faucet stem and washer along to the plumbing shop. Each model of faucet takes a different washer and O-ring. The same advice applies for kits to replace the ball-type faucet or for cartridge kits (sleeve or disc type.) **Remember:** Always shut off the water supply before going to work on faucets.

STYLE	PROBLEM	CAUSE	SOLUTION
Stem-Type Faucet	Water drips from faucet spout	Worn or damaged seat washer	Replace
		Corroded or worn seat	Regrind/ Replace
		Worn or damaged stem washer	Replace
		Worn stem	Replace
		Worn seat diaphragm	Replace
	Water leaks from handle base	Worn or damaged ''O'' rings	Replace
		Worn stem packing	Replace
	Faucet chatters or squeals when used	Loose or damaged stem screw	Tighten or replace
		Loose stem	Tighten
		Worn stem washer	Replace
Ball-Type Faucet	Water drips from faucet spout	Worn or damaged seats	Replace
		Weak springs	Replace
		Worn or damaged ball	Replace
	Leakage at spout handle	Worn cam	Replace
		Worn cam seal	Replace
		Loose or damaged adjusting ring	Tighten if loose; replace if damaged
	Leakage at bottom of spout handle	Worn or damaged body ''O'' rings	Replace
Cartridge Faucet	Water drips from faucet spout	Worn or damaged ''O'' rings	Replace
		Corroded or worn cartridge	Replace
	Leakage at faucet handle	Worn or damaged ''O'' rings	Replace
Disc Faucet	Water leaks from spout or handle	Worn or damaged disc seals	Replace

Troubleshooting guide.

Courtesy of PlumbShop.

Stem (Compression) Faucet

A common type of faucet is the compression, or stem-and-seat faucet. The compression faucet is commonly seen on double-handle sinks or bathtubs. These compression faucets have a neoprene washer at the base of the stem. Water control is achieved when the faucet washer is compressed against the faucet valve seat to seal it.

The first step is to shut off the water supply to the faucets. To disassemble the faucet, remove the screw holding the handle. Lift or pry gently upward to remove the faucet handle. Remove the retaining nut (or packing nut on some older faucet types) and then remove the stem from the faucet body. The washer is secured on the end of the stem by a stem screw. Remove the stem screw and pry out the old washer. Select a matching replacement washer from the washer assortment pack and install the new washer.

Before replacing the faucet stem, check the faucet seat to be sure it is smooth. If the seat feels rough to the touch, replace it. Use a seat wrench to remove and replace the seat at the bottom of the faucet body. If the seat is built into the faucet, rent a value-seat dresser. Slide the seat dresser into the faucet body and turn it clockwise to grind the seat smooth. Wipe out the metal filings with a cloth and reassemble the faucet.

The stem O-ring prevents water from leaking upward past the stem. To avoid duplicating repair efforts, always replace the O-rings at the same time you replace the faucet washer. Use a razor knife to cut the old O-ring off the stem. Apply plumber's faucet-and-valve grease (*use heatproof grease only*) to all moving parts. Then replace the O-ring.

On some older faucets the O-ring may be omitted, and there will be packing string or a packing washer on the stem instead. In this case, replace the packing string or washer. Reassemble the faucet and check for leaks. **Note:** Your bathtub may be served by wall-mounted compression faucets. Replacing the washers on these faucets is the same as above, but you will need an extension socket and reversible ratchet wrench to remove and replace the bonnet nut on these faucets. Often, the

Stem-Type Faucets

1. Shut off water supply valves then drain lines by turning both faucet handles on.

2. Pry off decorative cap on handle and remove screw holding handle.

3. Gently pry off handle with a screwdriver or use a faucet handle puller.

4. Use pliers or wrench to remove stem locknut/bonnet.

5. Depending on style of faucet, either unscrew stem or lift up to remove stem cartridge from faucet body.

6. To replace stem washer, remove brass screw (Fig. 3) and replace washer.

7. To resurface a worn or pitted faucet seat, insert faucet reseating tool as shown in Fig. 4. Press lightly and turn handle clockwise several times. Check for smoothness and be sure to remove filings with a damp cloth.

8. To remove an old seat, use faucet wrench (Fig. 5) and turn counterclockwise, then lift out. When installing a new seat, use pipe joint compound on outside threads of the seat to ensure a good seal.

9. Leaks at the faucet handle can usually be stopped by replacing the packing washer (Fig. 6). If you do not have or cannot get the correct washer, string packing (Fig. 7) can be wound around the stem clockwise, using 1-1/2 times as much thickness as would be required to fill the packing nut. When the nut is tightened, the packing compresses into solid form and acts as a seal.

10. Newer cartridge stems simply require the replacement of "O" rings to eliminate leaks.

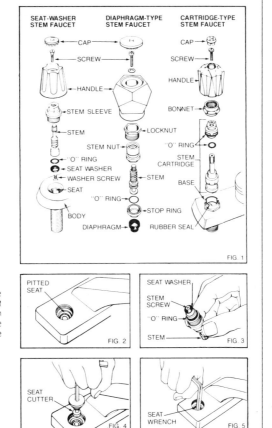

Stem-type faucet repair.

Courtesy of PlumbShop.

plumbing supply store will have a set of "loaner" extension sockets that you may rent/borrow for faucet repair.

Ball-Type Faucet

First, shut off the faucet water supply. Use the Allen wrench supplied with the repair kit to loosen the handle setscrew. To gain access to the adjusting ring, remove the faucet handle. Tighten the adjusting ring with adjustable pliers or the wrench that is supplied with the repair kit. To check the faucet, replace the faucet handle and turn on the water. If the faucet still leaks, remove the handle and unscrew the adjusting ring. Lift out the plastic cam, neoprene cam washer and the rotating ball. Using

a screwdriver, reach inside the faucet and remove the valve seats and springs. Lift the spout upward to remove it, and cut away the old O-rings. Coat the new O-ring with some heatproof grease and install the new O-ring. Reinstall the spout, then install new springs, valve seats, rotating ball, cam washer and cam. Replace the faucet handle and turn on the water.

Cartridge Faucet

There are two types of cartridge faucets. Fixing the *disc type* faucet is a simple repair. Shut off the water supply. Remove the index cap and handle screw, then lift up the faucet handle. Loosen the setscrew (with an Allen wrench) to remove the handle in-

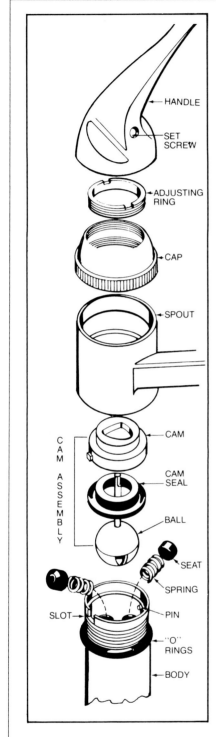

Ball-Type Faucet Repair

1. Shut off water supply valves then drain lines by turning faucet on.

2. Use an allen wrench to loosen the set screw holding the handle in place and remove handle.

3. Loosen and remove the adjusting ring by using the special wrench provided in the repair kit.

4. To remove cap, use pliers and turn counterclockwise. Protect cap finish with cloth.

5. Remove spout assembly.

6. Remove cam assembly by pulling up on ball shaft. You may need to use pliers.

7. Removing seats and springs is best done by inserting a pencil or sharp tool into the seat assembly and gently lifting it out. Check and clean inlet ports before replacing seats and springs.

8. To replace "O" rings on body, use a sharp tool to pry away from body. Roll new correct size "O" ring into place.

9. When reassembling, be sure to align slot in ball with pin in body and key on cam with slot in body.

10. Hand-tighten the cap, then screw adjusting ring into place with special wrench and replace handle. Turn on water and check for leaks. If necessary, further tighten adjusting ring.

Ball-type faucet repair.

Courtesy of PlumbShop.

sert, unscrew the dome cap and lift it off. Remove the cartridge mounting screws and lift out the cartridge. Insert the new cartridge and replace the mounting screws. Screw on the dome cap and replace the handle insert, handle and index cap.

To fix a leaking *sleeve-type* cartridge faucet, pry up the index cap and remove the lever (shut off the water supply first, of course). You must lift the lever to the maximum position to free the inner lever from the lip on the retaining nut. Use adjustable pliers to remove the retaining nut and the grooved collar (if one is present). Cut off and replace the O-rings, then replace the spout and retaining nut. Again holding the lever in its uppermost position, slip the flat edge of the inner lever over the rim of the retaining nut. Install the handle screw and the index cap.

AVOIDING PLUGGED DRAINS

A household drain system that is properly used and maintained should have few if any plugs or stoppages. A household drain is designed to carry away only waste water, human waste and kitchen waste (if the home is equipped with a garbage disposal). The key is never to use the drain system to dispose of other materials. Most plugged drains are caused by occupant error, usually by carelessly introducing materials never intended for sewer disposal into the drain. Below are some of the most common misuses of the drain/waste system.

Do not dispose of plaster or other patching materials in the sewer or drain. Plaster patching materials will harden in the drainpipes and clog them. Mix patching materials in plastic pails; let leftover materials set and harden in the pail, then flex the sides of the pail and dump out the hardened patch material. Wrap the lump of patch in newspapers and dispose of it in the trash.

Do not dump wastes such as coffee grounds down drains or toilets. If you have a kitchen garbage disposal unit, follow the manufacturer's directions for materials that can be put into the sewer via the disposal unit.

To avoid a plugged toilet, remember that toilet tissue is made to degrade in the sewer but other paper materials are not. Do not flush tampons, waste paper, soap wrappers or kitchen wastes down the toilet, because you may end up paying a plumber $60 an hour to come and remove it. Put bathroom-generated waste into a wastebasket, not into the toilet.

Garbage disposals should be operated with running water to flush down food particles and carry them into the main (large) drainpipes. To avoid fighting kitchen drain plugs, run plenty of water down the disposal to be sure that you have flushed all the waste out of the small sink-drainpipe into the larger main drainpipe.

Most bathtub drains are plugged by bits of soap and human hair. Do not use bar soap until it is reduced to a sliver, then flush the soap particles down the drain. The bits of soap help build stoppages in the drain. Dispose of the remnants of the soap bar in the wastebasket. Use a hair strainer over the drain in the bathtub.

Laundry plugs are caused by flushing bits of lint and thread down the laundry drain. Use a drain filter, the type that fits over the end of the washer drain hose, to prevent laundry lint from clogging the drains.

Do not wait until you have a sewer drain backup and a flooded basement to clean the main drain. Drain or sewer cleaning should be planned as routine maintenance, not as an emergency procedure to be done after your house or basement is already flooded and water damage has occurred. It's cheaper and less messy to have the drains cleaned *before* they back up. Your plumber can tell you how often the drains should be cleaned: Drains invaded by tree roots, or house drains used by large families, may need an annual cleaning, while the small family that is careful to keep foreign objects out of drains may delay drain cleaning for several years.

CLEANING A SINK SPRAYER

Over time, hard water can cause a sink sprayer head to become clogged and corroded. The primary problem with clogged sprayers is the mineral content of the water — either lime, calcium or iron. The most

Cartridge-Type Faucet Repair

1. Shut off water supply valves then drain lines by turning faucet on.

2. Pry off decorative cover and remove screw cap.

3. Pull spout assembly off.

4. Pull retainer clip from its slot.

5. Using pliers, lift cartridge out of body. Note position of cartridge ears so that when replacing, they are in identical position.

6. Remove "O" rings by prying away from body and rolling new ones into place, or replace entire cartridge.

7. Reverse procedure for reassembly.

Disc-Type Faucet Repair

1. Shut off water supply valves and drain lines by turning faucet on.

2. Lift handle up as far as possible and loosen set screw.

3. Lift handle off and unscrew cap.

4. Loosen screws holding ceramic disc cartridge in body and lift cartridge out.

5. On underside of cartridge are the set of seals that should be replaced. Check and clean inlet ports.

6. Reassemble by reversing above procedure, being sure cartridge holes align with inlet ports.

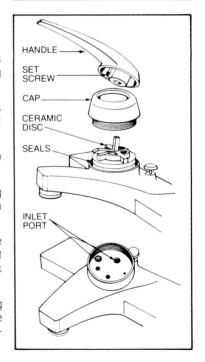

important point to remember for keeping plumbing fixtures looking new and working properly is to improve and maintain the quality of water in your home. If your water source is a private well, or if city water contains a high mineral content, you may want

Cartridge-type faucet repair.

Courtesy of PlumbShop.

Use a strainer such as this mesh model to block lint and laundry waste from clogging drains. Also use strainers at sink and bathtub drains. Have the main sewer drain cleaned periodically to prevent sewage backup and damage to the house or basement.

at your home center for doing tougher cleaning jobs. Some of these cleaners may contain phosphoric acid, which can damage materials such as polished aluminum or ceramic tile. Read and observe any label warnings about the use of household chemicals.

FIXING A BATHTUB STOPPER

Many modern bathtub stoppers have a pop-up feature, so that when you step on the stopper it seals the drain, and when you step again the drain plug pops up and open. But in older houses bathtubs may have stoppers that are operated by a lever connected to a lift assembly rod built into the tub overflow plate. The bathtub stopper and mechanism are exposed to a constant environment of water and soap scum, and if neglected the lever assembly may become corroded and eventually inoperable. To ensure good operation the stopper should be disassembled periodically, then cleaned and lubricated. Wipe the stopper clean of soap residue and hair to ensure that the stopper seals the drain.

If the lever breaks or seizes, you can buy replacement parts for most bathtub stopper assemblies. Because the assemblies differ by manufacturer, parts are not interchangeable and often you cannot find replacement parts at home centers. To obtain repair parts you must seek out a plumbing dealer who handles your brand of fixtures.

not only to soften the water but to install mineral filters in your water supply line to improve the water quality.

Cleaning a clogged sprayer head is an easy task. First, turn off the water supply to the sprayer head. Disconnect the sprayer head from the hose, laying out any parts in the order you remove them. There is a screw cover in the spray nozzle: Use a small screwdriver to pry off the cover. To gain access to the seat and perforated disc inside the sprayer head, remove the small screw inside the nozzle. Use a toothbrush to clean the small parts of the sprayer head.

Some stubborn minerals such as lime *may* yield to an overnight soaking in ordinary vinegar. Buy a lime cleaner chemical

CLEANING A SHOWER HEAD

Depending on the degree of hardness and the mineral content of your home water supply, lime or other minerals can plug the tiny holes in shower heads. The first line of defense for protecting plumbing fixtures is maintaining good water quality. An early clue indicating poor water quality—or a high lime or iron content—is stained or rusty bathroom fixtures and faucets. Install a water softener and mineral filter if plumbing fixtures show signs of excessive mineral buildup.

To clean a plugged shower head, first remove the shower head from the water pipe. In most cases you should be able to unscrew the shower head with your bare hands. If the shower head is so tight that a pipe wrench is required for removal, wrap masking tape around the shower head to protect it from being scratched by the wrench jaws.

Carefully remove the shower head; use steel wool or a scrub pad to clean it. Lime removal products such as Lime Away, available from your local home center, can be used to soak away any lime or mineral buildup. Or you can soak the parts in warm vinegar to remove the mineral buildup.

REPLACING A BATHTUB SPOUT

Many bathtub/shower plumbing setups have a diverter valve in the waterspout. To fill the bathtub, the diverter valve is pushed down and water flows into the bathtub. To use the shower, the knob is pulled upward to shut a diverter valve in the spout, so that the water is turned, or diverted, to flow upward into the shower head.

With use the diverter valve may become clogged by mineral buildup or corrosion. When this happens the valve may not close completely, so part of the water volume flows into the tub and part of the water is diverted to the shower head. This can result in an unsatisfactory volume of water through the shower head.

To remedy this problem, remove the defective diverter spout and replace it with a new spout. Use a pipe wrench or large pliers with adjustable jaws to remove the old spout. To avoid damaging the finish on the spout, wrap it with a thick layer of masking tape before turning the spout with the wrench or pliers. If the spout has been in place for many years the threads on the spout and the water pipe may be corroded, so the spout may be difficult to remove. To avoid having the tool slip and damage the tub or tile, be sure the jaws of the wrench or pliers grip the spout firmly, and carefully apply pressure on the tool.

After removing the defective spout, use a wire brush or steel wool to clean the threads on the water pipe. Apply a thin film of plumber's grease to the pipe threads to ease installation of the new spout. New diverter spouts have a molded and threaded plastic sleeve inside the metal spout. The plastic sleeve makes installation easier, and will also prevent rust or corrosion on the pipe or spout threads, ensuring that future spout replacement will be a much easier process.

REPLACING A SINK TRAP

Hidden away under most plumbing fixtures, installed in the drainpipe, is a U- or J-shaped pipe called a *trap*. A trap performs several functions. The first and most important function is to trap and retain water in the lower bend. The trapped water blocks the drainpipe so that odors and sewer gases cannot flow back through the drain and into the house. The trap also provides a first line of defense against plugged drains by catching any materials that might form a plug farther down the drain where it would be more difficult to reach and to remove. Traps are also easily removed for access to the piping and plug if a plugged drain does occur.

Because metal drain traps are constantly full of water, they are constantly exposed to rust and corrosion, and are thus subject to rust-out and will require replacement. Today's plastic traps are more resistant to corrosion and failure, and may literally last forever, but in time the metal traps will fail and will require replacement.

To replace a trap the only tool you need is a pipe wrench or a pair of adjustable-jaw pliers. Some metal and plastic traps may be interchangeable, but to ensure a good match and avoid frustration it is usually easier to replace a metal trap with metal or a plastic trap with plastic.

REPAIRING A RUNNING TOILET

After the toilet is flushed the flapper ball falls back to prevent water from flowing into the toilet bowl. The toilet tank refills with water via the toilet flush valve. A float inside the tank rises as the tank fills, and when the water reaches the proper level in the tank the rising float shuts off a water valve. The toilet tank is now filled, waiting for the next flush action. When the flush lever is pushed, the flapper ball is lifted to open the hole and the water flows into the toilet bowl to flush it.

The flapper ball is made of rubber or plastic. If the flapper ball becomes worn or deteriorated it may not seal the tank completely, and some amount of water may leak past it. This not only wastes water, but is a nuisance because of the sound of water continuously running into the toilet bowl.

If you have a ballcock/float-rod toilet, the water flow into the valve seat is blocked by a tank ball. On newer toilets the water flow is blocked by a flapper ball. If you have a toilet that runs continuously, first check the chain that connects the flush handle to the tank or flapper ball. If the

chain is too short it may not let the flapper ball close completely. The cure is to lengthen the chain so the ball can close completely. If the chain seems the proper length but there is excess chain hanging below the flapper ball, the extra chain may be dropping between the flapper ball and the flush valve seat. Use wirecutting pliers to cut off the excess chain.

If the flapper ball appears to be worn, cracked or coated with minerals or other residue, replace it.

The flapper ball is easy to replace. First, remove the old flapper ball and discard it. Then install the new flapper ball. On older ballcock/float-rod toilets you simply unscrew the tank ball from the threaded lift wire and then screw the new float ball onto the lift wire.

REPLACING A TOILET FLUSH VALVE

Older toilet hardware may be made of brass and may include a ballcock, float rod and float ball. These brass units are quite expensive. New toilet flush valves are inexpensive, made of plastic, and have a float cup that encircles the ballcock shank. This

Turn the threaded base of the flush valve to adjust the height.

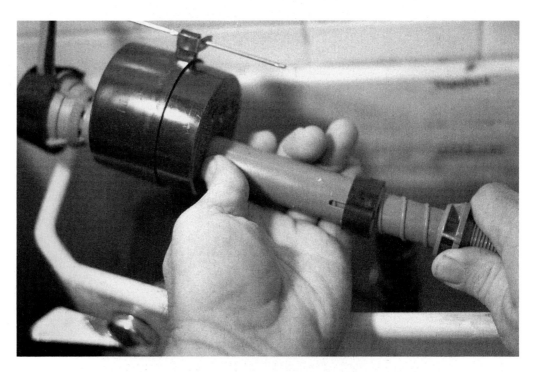

eliminates the float rod and float cup. If the old ballcock is not working well, replace it with the plastic model for about $10.

To replace the flush valve, first shut off the water supply at the valve under the toilet tank. Now flush the toilet to empty both the toilet tank and bowl. Use a large sponge to remove any water remaining in the toilet tank. Place a pail under the water supply pipe to the toilet tank. Use a wrench with adjustable jaws to loosen the water supply pipe and the retaining nut that holds the flush valve to the toilet tank. Remove the old flush valve or ballcock hardware and dispose of it.

Now set the new flush valve into the hole in the toilet tank. Secure it to the toilet tank with the plastic retaining nut and tighten. To adjust the water level in the toilet tank, pinch the spring clip on the pull rod and adjust the float cup position on the ballcock shank. (To lower the water level in the toilet tank, for example, adjust the float cup downward on the shank.)

CURING A LAZY TOILET DRAIN

The toilet may seem to flush properly, and then one day the water rises to the rim of

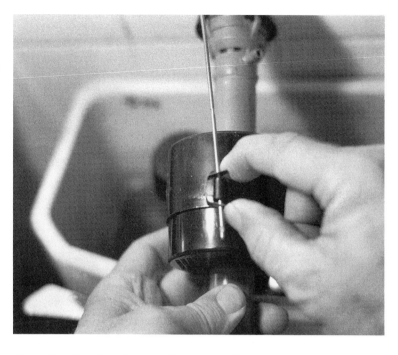

the toilet bowl and goes down in a lazy spiral. You check for a partial plug in the toilet drainpipe, using a toilet plunger or a snake. The toilet flushes in the same lazy way.

The problem may be a mineral buildup inside the toilet bowl. When the toilet is flushed, the water runs into concealed channels within the bowl. Water runs out

To adjust the level of the float, pinch the spring clip on the side of the flush valve.

Clip the flush tube to the overflow pipe in the toilet tank. Adjust the chain or strap connecting the flush lever to the flapper ball.

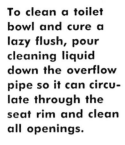

To clean a toilet bowl and cure a lazy flush, pour cleaning liquid down the overflow pipe so it can circulate through the seat rim and clean all openings.

from holes under the rim of the bowl to rinse the sides. Also, at the front edge of the bowl you will see a small entry hole. This hole may become plugged with minerals from the water, so that the water flow is restricted or the water velocity is reduced. Then the toilet will flush with a lazy drain. Reach into the toilet bowl and run a finger into the hole at the bowl front. If there is significant mineral buildup you can feel the blockage with your finger.

To cure this problem, use a small screwdriver or chisel to chip away the mineral buildup. After scraping the perimeter of the hole, flush the toilet to see if water flow has been restored. If so, your problem is solved. There are also drain cleaners available to clean out the channels inside the bowl, far up where you cannot reach with a scraper. To clean out the interior water channels of a toilet you must pour the cleaner into the overflow pipe in the toilet tank. The chemical cleaners often contain acid, so read the label and handle such products with care.

STOPPING WATER HAMMER

The water pressure in municipal water systems may reach as high as 90-pounds-per-square-inch. When water is running, the water is moving at this high pressure and velocity at the faucet, so if the faucet is abruptly turned off the water may stop with an audible bang. This water stoppage can be especially abrupt at the solenoid shutoff valve of an automatic washing machine, and can produce a particularly loud bang. The common term for this phenomenon is *water hammer*. Water hammer not only makes an annoying noise but it also can cause water pipe vibration and can loosen or crack pipe fittings and joints.

The cure for water hammer is to install an air chamber, or water hammer muffler, at the end of the pipe run. You should have mufflers on both the hot and cold water supply pipes. Install the mufflers as close as possible to the water supply faucets where the water hammer is occurring. The water hammer muffler may be a simple closed copper tube, or it may be a plastic ball that encloses a rubber bladder. In either type of muffler, or air chamber, the water column is pushed against trapped air. Unlike water, air can be compressed. The water in the pipe compresses the air and cushions the shock of water stoppage, ending the water hammer.

To install the copper water hammer muffler, cut out a section of the water supply pipe and solder a *T* fitting in the line. Before soldering, use fine sandpaper to clean both ends of the pipes and inside the connector or fixture sockets. Then use an acid flux to clean the surfaces to be soldered. Use a non-lead solder to avoid having lead problems in the water. Heat the surfaces to be soldered with a propane torch. Apply the solder wire to the joint, watching to make sure the solder flows into and seals the joints.

To prevent all of the air from being driven out of the chamber by the water, the copper muffler must be installed vertically, so the top is up, not horizontally. Solder the air chamber in place to complete the installation.

If your project will not permit installation of a vertical copper air chamber you can install a plastic model instead. The plastic water hammer muffler contains a rubber bladder. Air is trapped inside the muffler between the plastic bulb and the air bladder. In this model the air cannot be pushed out; the muffler can be installed in any position, even upside down or horizontal to the water pipe.

MAINTAINING THE WATER HEATER

Water heaters often perform heavy-duty service year after year; a few simple steps can extend the heater's life and keep it operating properly.

The first indication of water heater failure may be no hot water, or you may see water running out from under the heater. These are sure signs that the heater needs attention or replacement.

If your water supply is hard (if the water has a high mineral content), minerals or sediment that accumulate at the bottom of the water heater can insulate the water from the burner's heat, extending recovery time for the water heater and wasting energy. Place a plastic pail under the drain valve near the bottom of your water heater, or attach a garden hose to it, then turn on

To eliminate mineral buildup, periodically drain water from the bottom of the water heater. The frequency of this step depends on the water quality.

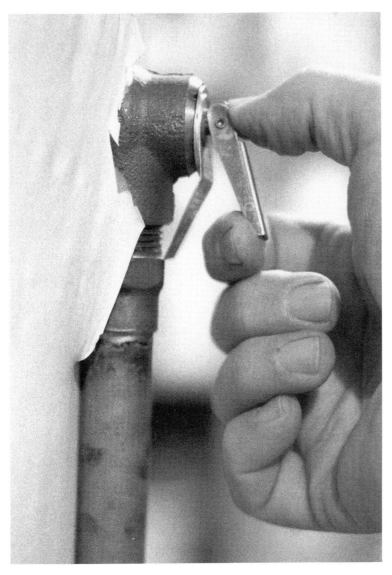

The lever and pipe at the side of the heater are for emergency pressure relief to avoid a steam explosion. Place a pail under the pipe and test the pressure relief valve to be sure it is working.

the water and let it run until it is clear and free from any sediment.

On the side of the water heater you will find a water tube and a small valve. This is the pressure release valve, designed to open if the heater malfunctions to prevent dangerous steam buildup or possibly an explosion. To be sure the valve is still operable, place a catch pail under the end of the relief tube and hold up the relief valve until water runs out of the tube.

When the water heater's gas burner is on, light a match and hold it under the hood of the exhaust vent at the top of the unit. If the vent is open the flame from the match should flicker upward. The hood and vent pipe are secured in the larger fur-

nace duct pipe by one or two small sheet-metal screws. If your heater is several years old, remove the vent pipe and clean it, then reinstall it. Remember, to ensure that no one will be burned or scalded by hot water from the heater, keep your thermostat set at or below 110°F (43°C).

REPAIRING WASHING MACHINE HOSE VALVES

Two washer hose valves (stem faucets) control the water supply to the automatic washing machine. These faucets are used to shut off the water supply to the washing machine during repair or replacement of the machine. You should also use the washer hose valves to shut off the water when the washing machine is not in use. If the hose valves are left open full time the constant water pressure may cause the rubber hoses to break and flood the laundry area. For this reason you should shut off the faucets when the wash cycle is finished. To ensure that the hoses do not rupture, replace them every three to five years.

In time, the hose valves will develop leaks, either through the faucet spout or around the stem. Because the heat from hot water will deteriorate the stem washer faster than cold water, the hot water faucet usually begins to leak first. However, it doesn't pay to repair one hose valve at a time. Because you have to turn off the water supply at the meter to repair the faucets, it's best to repair both hot and cold hose faucets while you already have the proper tools and replacement washers handy and the water turned off.

For a guide on how stem faucets work see the stem faucet illustration in "Repairing Leaking Faucets" (page 51). To take the hose faucets apart for repairs use a pipe wrench or adjustable pliers to turn and loosen the nut on the top of the faucet. With the nut removed you can pull out the faucet stem.

On the bottom end of the faucet stem, secured by a single small screw, you will find a replaceable washer. Because washer

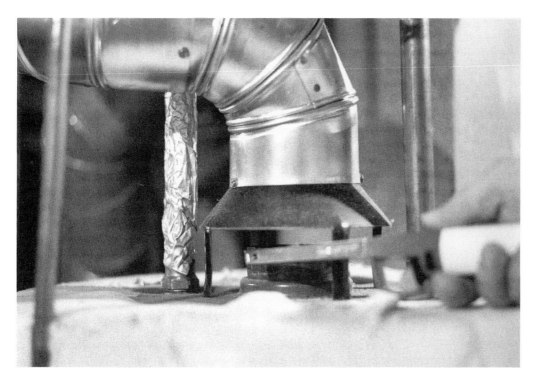

Test the water heater vent to be sure it is open. While the heater burner is on, hold a lighter or match under the vent hood and be sure that there is an up-draft, indicating an open vent.

sizes vary by faucet type and manufacturer, it's best to buy a package of assorted washer sizes to be sure you have the right one. Remove the screw and replace the washer with one the same size.

At the top of the stem, under the retaining nut, you will find an O-ring or a graphite-coated stem packing. Remove the old O-ring or packing and replace it. To test for leaks, reassemble the faucet and turn the water on.

Plumbing Checklist

- Determine the faucet type and manufacturer before repairing a leaky faucet.
- Use the household drain system properly, not for disposal of plaster, coffee grounds, paper or other items.
- Plan to clean drains and sewers routinely.
- Maintain and repair bathtub stoppers, shower heads, bathtub spouts and sink traps regularly.
- Replace or adjust the flapper ball to repair a running toilet.
- Fix a lazy toilet drain by clearing out mineral buildup.
- Install a water hammer muffler at the end of a pipe run to stop water hammer.
- Perform regular maintenance and checkups on your water heater to extend its life and performance.

MAINTAINING THE SEPTIC SYSTEM

If you have a vacation retreat or own a house out beyond the reach of municipal utility services you may have your own sewage or septic system. In a septic system household waste generated by the bathroom, kitchen and laundry — 99 percent of which is water — runs through a drainpipe into a septic tank. Nonliquids such as human waste and paper settle out in the tank. As the solids settle out, liquids in the tank may flow into a second tank or into a second compartment within a single tank. When settling has occurred the liquid sewage flows into a series of seepage pipes — pipes with holes that permit the liquids to flow out and be absorbed into the soil or a gravel seepage bed. This is sometimes called a *leach field* because the liquids leach (are absorbed) into the soil.

Light or sandy soils have no difficulty in handling the liquid seepage. Heavy or clay soils that cannot easily absorb the liquids may be dug out, the excavated trench may be filled with gravel to form a leach field, then the trenches are backfilled with topsoil and seeded or sodded over.

The size of the septic tank varies according to the size of the house: Any house up to two bedrooms will have a minimum 750-gallon septic tank; a three-bedroom house a 1,000-gallon septic tank; and a four-bedroom house might have a 1,200-gallon septic tank. If you are buying a house, try to find out the size of the septic system, to ensure that the system is large enough to handle the needs of your family. The size of the septic tank should be on record at the local building department.

A septic system that is properly built and maintained should last for years. Natural bacterial action will help break down the solids into sludge and scum that can be pumped out by septic service companies; waste liquids will seep into the soil in the leach field; and sewer gases will pass back up the septic drainpipe and be exhausted by the sewer vent system of the house. Depending on how much waste your household generates, have your septic tank pumped every three to five years. The septic serviceman can advise you on how often you should have the tank pumped.

The following checklist will help you maintain your septic system and avoid serious and expensive problems:

• Reduce the amount of waste your septic system must handle. Fix leaking faucets or running toilets that waste water and overload the septic system. Water-saving devices such as low-flow shower heads and low-volume toilets are a real plus to reduce water usage and avoid overworking the system.

• Don't use your toilet as a waste disposal system. Only toilet tissue should be flushed down the toilet.

• Avoid using "miracle" chemicals that are advertised to increase bacterial action in the septic system. Bacterial action will naturally occur in a properly built system. Putting the wrong chemicals in the septic system may kill the natural bacterial action that must be present to break down solids. Use chemical or bacterial additives only on the advice of your serviceman.

• In the laundry or bathroom avoid using cleaning or bleaching chemicals that might interfere with natural bacterial action in the system. Look for products labeled "safe for septic tanks."

• Don't neglect pumping the septic tank until problems appear. An overloaded septic system can result in solids entering the seepage pipes and plugging them. You may then have to rebuild your leach fields.

CHAPTER 4

HEATING AND AIR CONDITIONING

A flame burning in a furnace is what fire officials refer to as a "friendly fire," one that is helpful. But because any flame can potentially become a "hostile fire," most utility companies recommend that the homeowner limit his labors to regular cleaning and maintenance procedures and leave repairs to the professionals. Those maintenance procedures that can be safely performed by the homeowner are covered here.

Depending on where you live, you can have a professional furnace inspection and tuneup done each fall for between $50 and $100. The service professional will inspect the heat exchanger for signs of dangerous leaks, clean and adjust the burner, and observe the general operation of the furnace to be sure it will perform faithfully and safely through the next heating season.

MAINTAINING THE FURNACE

Each manufacturer supplies an owner's manual with their furnaces, because furnace maintenance requirements vary by model and manufacturer. Consult the manual for specific maintenance instructions on your particular furnace. General instructions for furnace maintenance include inspecting the disposable dust filter monthly during furnace operation (heating *and* air conditioning) and replacing the filter when it's dirty. Although neglecting the filter can turn your forced-air furnace into a dust machine, this simple task is often

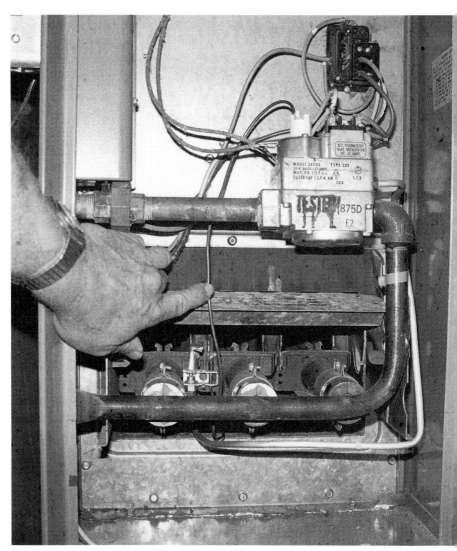

The thermocouple, indicated by the index finger, connects the furnace controls to the pilot light bracket. The pilot's heat on the thermocouple generates a small electric current that opens the gas supply valve. If the pilot light will not stay lit, replace the thermocouple.

neglected. Replacing a dirty filter not only keeps the furnace and ducts clean, but also will reduce cleaning and decorating requirements by helping to keep the walls, ceilings and furnishings clean.

Clean air registers once a year and have the furnace ducts cleaned by pros every two years. To prevent rust damage to the furnace cabinet, dehumidify or ventilate a damp basement or other furnace area. To further protect against rust, apply a coat of paste auto wax to the furnace cabinet.

The blower motor of your furnace may be permanently lubricated, or it may need periodic oiling. Check with the owner's manual or the manufacturer to find the lubrication requirements for your particular furnace. Use a flexible-spout engineer's oiler to pump a couple of drops of 30-weight motor oil into each oiling port. While you have the blower housing out of the furnace, clean the blower fan; use the upholstery nozzle on the vacuum cleaner. Then replace the blower unit.

A furnace that is not properly adjusted can not only burn inefficiently but can also fail to draft properly so there is a danger of carbon monoxide poisoning. For maximum safety and efficiency have the furnace burner and controls cleaned and adjusted by a professional at the start of each heating season.

LIGHTING A FURNACE PILOT LIGHT

To keep the home fires burning you should have the furnace burner assembly cleaned and adjusted by a professional. Remove the front door of the furnace and check the flame on the burners. If the flames are yellow or orange, rather than blue, the gas/oxygen mix needs adjustment. Look under the chimney and around the burner unit for accumulations of rust or scale. These may indicate problems with the burner or the heat exchanger. Any unusual buildup of condensation on window glass in cold weather can also be a signal that products of combustion from the furnace burner

may not be exhausting properly. If it has been more than two years since a service-person checked the furnace, have the job done before the start of the next heating season. A properly adjusted burner will conserve fuel, so you may save enough in fuel costs to more than pay for the cost of servicing.

Some pilot lights are called standing, or continuous flame, pilot lights, and some are electronic. If the standing pilot light on your furnace will not stay lit it may need cleaning, or the problem may be a defective *thermocouple*. Remove the furnace door and you will see a small metal control box. The thermocouple is a thin copper tube that runs from the control (valve) box down to a clip adjacent to the pilot light.

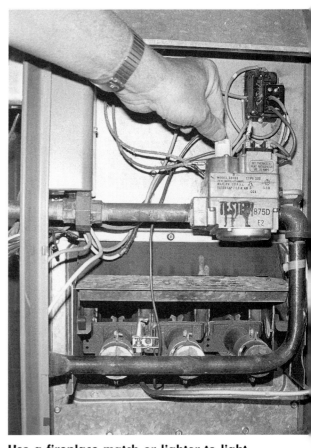

Use a fireplace match or lighter to light the pilot light. With the flame already lit, turn the knob to "Pilot" and hold the knob down. When the pilot ignites, continue to hold the knob down for a full minute before releasing it. The pilot should stay lit.

The heat from the pilot light generates a small electric current through the thermocouple, and the electric current opens the gas supply valve. If the thermocouple is defective it will conduct no current and the pilot light will not stay lit. Have the thermocouple replaced.

If the pilot light loses its flame at the end of the burn cycle, turn down the thermostat and relight the pilot light. The directions for lighting the pilot light are usually prominently posted on the door or front cover of the furnace. Turn the thermostat back up, and the burner should come on and run until the thermostat is satisfied.

If the pilot light goes out when the burner goes off, suspect one of two possible causes. First, the thermocouple may be set too low in its bracket, so the flame of the pilot light does not hit the thermocouple tip directly. Carefully try to push the bulb, or end, of the thermocouple up in the bracket so the pilot flame will touch it. Relight the pilot and let the furnace burner cycle. If the pilot stays lit after you have adjusted the thermocouple, you have solved the problem. If adjusting the thermocouple doesn't help and the pilot still goes out when the burner goes off, have a serviceperson check the gas pressure and clean the pilot light.

TUNING FURNACE DUCTS

Maybe you've installed insulation and weatherstripping but the heating bills are still too high. Or now that the children are grown and on their own you have unused bedrooms that are still being heated. Or some rooms in your house are too warm, while others are too cold. The solution to all these problems is to be sure the dampers in your furnace ducts are adjusted or "tuned" to deliver heat where it is needed most.

When the heating mechanic installed your forced-air furnace he adjusted or tuned the dampers in your air ducts. Without knowing the details of your future life-

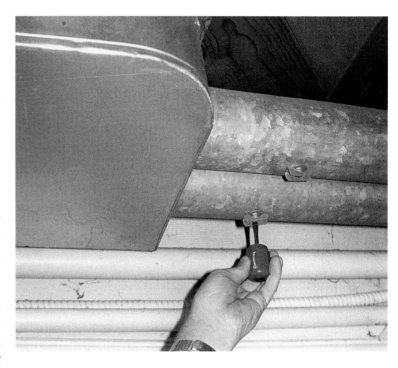

style or your family's living patterns, the best the installer could do was to try to see that conditioned air was evenly distributed to all the rooms in the house. But if you have not adjusted the duct dampers to meet changing needs you may be living with the damper adjustments chosen by the heating mechanic, using only the wall- or floor-mounted air registers to control the flow of warm air in winter and cool air in summer. If you are not satisfied with the distribution of the air supply in your house, retune the duct dampers to satisfy your needs. For example, if you have seldom-used extra bedrooms you may elect to shut the duct dampers to those rooms.

One point of caution: Thinking they can reduce energy consumption and expense by not heating or cooling a room or rooms, some people close the wall air registers. The truth is that if you move the conditioned air down any duct but close the register, you have already paid to condition it but you are not fully using it. Rather than simply closing the wall registers, shut the dampers in those ducts that serve unused rooms so that the conditioned air is not delivered where it is not needed. Then be sure the duct dampers are fully opened to

Check your heat ducts where they exit from the furnace to find the duct dampers. Adjust the dampers until the desired heat distribution is achieved.

rooms where conditioned air is needed.

Tuning furnace ducts is especially effective when the unused spaces are on other floors, i.e., second-floor bedrooms or basement space. For example, close duct dampers to any unused bedrooms or guest rooms. Rooms that are nearest to the furnace receive the hottest air: Close the dampers to those rooms nearest to the furnace, and fully open the dampers in ducts that supply the rooms most distant from the furnace.

The first step to duct tuning is to locate all furnace ducts and to identify which duct serves which room or area. The furnace air ducts in most homes are accessible from the basement or crawl space. **Note:** In some newer homes dampers have been eliminated in the furnace ducts, so the only adjustment available is via the registers. Check the ducts to find the dampers, and check each damper to see whether it is open or shut. On the duct dampers there may be locking nuts that must be loosened in order to adjust the dampers. The damper shafts usually have screwdriver slots for easy adjustment. To adjust the dampers use a slot screwdriver to turn them, then tighten the locking nuts to lock the dampers firmly in position.

MAINTAINING A HUMIDIFIER

Warm or hot air can hold more moisture (humidity) than cold air, so when the furnace is heating the air during cold weather, indoor relative humidity falls and the air becomes dry. For maximum personal comfort, indoor humidity levels should be maintained between 30 and 50 percent year around. In cold weather, however, indoor humidity levels may drop to 13 percent, or about the same level found in Death Valley. When indoor humidity levels drop too low the plaster on the walls and ceilings may crack, wood joints can open up in furniture or trim molding, and when you touch something after walking across carpeted floors you can get annoying static electric shocks. When you add in personal

discomforts such as itchy, dry skin and dry throat and nasal passages you can understand the need for humidification.

Types of humidifiers available include drum, wick, impeller, ultrasonic and steam (or warm mist) models. Humidifiers also vary in capacity: Tell your dealer how much floor space you have, or consult the manufacturer's recommendations to be sure you buy a humidifier large enough to meet your needs.

To establish proper indoor humidification, start by setting humidistat levels at around 30 percent. If you feel more humidity is needed, gradually turn the controls up until the glass in the windows begins to fog over in cold winter weather. Then turn the humidifier controls down until the windows are free of condensation. If humidity levels are left so high that moisture constantly condenses on window glass the moisture can run down the window and damage the window finish or sash.

Your humidifier may be a console or portable unit or it may be mounted in the furnace duct directly above the furnace. Water is automatically delivered to duct-mounted humidifiers via a water supply tube. Portable or console units can be filled from a pail or from a fill hose that can be connected to a faucet. The fill hose is supplied with the unit. Supply the humidifier with pure water that has been softened or filtered to keep the unit clean and working well. If you live in an area where the water is hard or contains lots of iron, buy bottled water for use in your portable humidifier.

Change the water daily in portable or console-type humidifiers, because water supports growth of bacteria and mold. Clean the unit every three days, washing the interior of the water reservoir with hydrogen peroxide. The peroxide will kill any mold and bacterial growth.

INSTALLING HIGH-EFFICIENCY AIR FILTERS

Most forced-air furnaces have an inexpensive fiber glass filter mounted in the cold air return. This filter is called a dust-stop filter. As the furnace blower motor moves air through the ducts and the house the air picks up all sorts of pollutants, so the dust-stop filter is used to filter out large particles of dust, lint, grease or pollen. These dust-stop filters are used primarily to keep dust and dirt out of the furnace ducts and blower unit. Dust-stop filters will not filter out smaller airborne particles such as smoke, most pollens, viral matter, mildew spores or smaller dust particles.

Experts estimate that 99 percent of indoor air pollutants are microscopic in size, too small to be filtered out by cheap dust-stop filters. If you suffer from allergies, sinus problems or bronchial ailments you should consider installing a high-efficiency furnace filter.

Inexpensive dust-stop filters can trap particles that are larger than 100 microns in diameter. More efficient filters, called media air filters, can screen out the larger particles and can also trap smaller particles, as small as 0.5 microns, on fibers inside the filters. This is a great improvement in indoor air quality for those who have any allergy or respiratory problems. Media air filters can be purchased for $8 to $10 each from your heating supply dealer or hardware store. If your dealer does not have media filters in stock, ask him to special-order them for you. Some highly efficient electronic filters can cost upward of $1,000 (professionally installed), but be aware that if your physician orders such measures for you or for a family member you may be able to take the electronic filter as a medical deduction on your income taxes.

Also, certain manufacturers are offering new thinner electronic air cleaners that can be installed by the do-it-yourselfer and fit easily into the furnace cold air duct.

To keep the forced-air furnace blower and ductwork clean, along with your home's interior, change dust-stop filters monthly. For those with allergies or bronchial conditions, consider installing a supe-

rior media air filter or an electronic air filter for the best protection.

MAINTAINING HOT WATER RADIATORS

Hot water/radiant heating has been a popular residential heating choice for many decades, and for good reason. Hot water radiant heating is an even, draft-free and economical method for heating a house. Older radiant heating systems consist of a boiler (where water is heated by a burner), insulated distribution piping to deliver the hot water to radiators and to return the cooled water to the boiler for reheating, and heavy cast-iron radiators that can absorb the heat from the water and radiate it

More efficient air filters, called media filters, can be used to replace your furnace dust filters. A more costly solution is to install an electronic air cleaner such as the Electro-air shown. This model can remove airborne pollutant particles down to .01 micron in size — small enough to filter out smoke.

Photo courtesy of White-Rogers Division of Emerson Electric Co.

into the house. This type of hot water heating might be a gravity-style unit, meaning the heating and cooling of the water causes it to move. Or the system might include a low-volume circulating pump. Newer hot water radiant systems consist of a water boiler and a delivery system of copper piping, with aluminum fins to disperse the heat from the copper pipe at baseboard radiators. These copper pipe/aluminum fin radiators, unlike the heavy cast-iron radiators, have little capacity to absorb and radiate the heat from the hot water. High-speed pumps must be used to circulate the water swiftly through the radiant baseboard system.

Regardless of the type of hot water heating system you have, the most common maintenance chore is to check the radiators for trapped air. Air trapped in the radiator chambers prevents water from flowing into the chambers. If you have cold radiators in some rooms you must use a slot screwdriver or a bleeder key to loosen the screw of the bleeder valve and remove, or "bleed," the air out of the chamber. Simply turn the bleeder screw on the valve until you hear a sputtering or hissing noise. That noise is the sound of air escaping from the radiator. Leave the bleeder valve open until only hot water runs out, with no sound of hissing or bubbling. A steady stream of water indicates that all the air is out of the radiator and only water remains. Close the bleeder screw on the valve and give the radiator time to warm up. Then check the radiator to be sure it is working properly. **Tip:** Some of the old cast-iron radiators settle and are not level. These radiators often do not heat properly. Heat can sometimes be restored by lifting a radiator up and shimming the legs so the unit is level.

REPLACING A STEAM RADIATOR VENT

If your heating system is radiant steam, most problems may be solved by replacing one of two components. One of these components is the steam vent, found on the top corner of the radiator's outside cell. The second component is the steam-trap bellows, found at the bottom corner of the radiator where the radiator outlet pipe and condensate pipe meet.

The steam vent is a cone-shaped device at the top of the radiator. Over time the vent may become clogged with minerals from the water. In an emergency you may be able to clean away the mineral residue and open the steam vent, but the best permanent cure is to replace the plugged steam vent with a new one. Turn off the inlet valve to the radiator, then unscrew the steam vent. In most cases you will not need a wrench, but will be able to remove the steam vent by hand. After removing the old steam vent, coat the threads of the new steam vent with antiseize compound to make the installation and future removal easier.

If a steam radiator makes a pounding noise and does not heat properly the problem is caused by the steam-trap bellows. As steam cools and condenses in the radiator the steam trap collects the water and returns it to the condensate tank. The steam-trap bellows is sensitive to heat and will open to let cold water return to the condensate tank, but will snap shut to trap the hot steam in the radiator. If the bellows fails and does not shut, the steam escapes from the radiator along with the condensate. This escaping steam produces a pounding noise; without the steam the radiator will fail to heat properly.

Use a 12-inch pipe wrench or adjustable pliers to remove the cap from the steam-trap. Then use adjustable pliers to unscrew the bellows from the cap. Because the replacement bellows may not look exactly like the old bellows it is best to take the old bellows along to the heating supply dealer to be sure to get a replacement bellows that fits. Lubricate the threads with antiseize compound, both on the thermal bellows and on the steam-trap cap, to ease installation and future removal.

SEALING CRACKS AT ELECTRICAL OUTLETS

If you've done all the obvious insulating and weatherstripping to reduce heating and air conditioning costs, there are still possible savings through attention to smaller details such as sealing the little cracks that can permit air infiltration and add up to big losses of conditioned air. The first rule for stopping air infiltration is not to ignore small savings. Seal up any crack you can find. If the crack is between two nonmoving materials, such as siding and window or door trim, caulk the crack tight. If the crack is between a nonmoving material (such as a door or window frame) and a moving component (such as a door or a window) install weatherstripping. Sealing up all the small cracks, such as those around electrical outlets, can also help reduce heating and cooling bills.

To avoid electrical shock, first turn off the power to the outlet. Then remove the outlet cover. Fill any cracks between the plaster or wallboard and the outlet box with spackle or taping compound. Use a putty knife or a wet fingertip to fill and smooth the cracks. Let the patch material dry, then position foam plastic insulation covers over the receptacle or switch. Install the insulation covers at all electrical outlets that are on outside walls to stop air infiltration and to conserve energy.

As a final step, fill unused slots in receptacles with small plastic outlet covers. The plastic covers have a pair of prongs that fit into receptacle slots and seal air out.

Heating Checklist

- Check the owner's manual for maintenance requirements for your furnace.
- Clean air registers once a year; have ducts cleaned by pros every two years.
- Lubricate the furnace's blower motor if indicated by the manufacturer.
- Check the burner flame for proper adjustment.
- Tune furnace ducts for optimum efficiency.
- Consider installing a high-efficiency air filter.
- Check hot water radiators for trapped air; bleed as necessary.
- Seal cracks at electrical outlets to prevent unnecessary heat loss.

MAINTAINING CENTRAL AIR CONDITIONING

The first rule to remember is to save all owner's manuals and warranty papers for household appliances and equipment. This will ensure that you have an accurate guide for servicing major equipment. New furnaces and air conditioners will operate with a minimum of maintenance, but there are steps you can take to be sure the units are functioning properly and are ready for the summer season.

The first rule on forced-air furnace/air conditioning equipment is to replace the furnace filter frequently to ensure that dust and grime are removed. If the filter is neglected the dirt will not only foul up the blower motor and ducts of the furnace system, but will also become a dirt machine, distributing dirt over walls, ceilings and furnishings in your house. Don't neglect filter replacement.

Outside the house, usually setting on a concrete pad, is the air conditioner compressor unit. The fan on the compressor pulls in outdoor air to cool the unit. Along with the air the fan may pull in dust, insects and other debris, clogging the fins on the compressor. To clean the compressor, remove the sheet metal retaining screws that hold the top on the compressor cabinet, then lift up the top for access inside the cabinet.

Inside the metal compressor cabinet you will see copper tubing fitted with aluminum fins. Like the radiator in your car, heat from the house is pulled into this radiator unit, and the blower fan moves air over the radiator assembly to dissipate the heat. The blower fan has to work harder to extract heat from dirty or clogged radiator fins. Us-

To clean the air conditioner compressor unit, remove the top and use a spray nozzle to wash dirt from the coils and fins.

ing a nozzle and garden hose, spray away the debris from the compressor radiator, spraying from the inside toward the outside of the compressor cabinet. As you spray the inside, keep watch on the outside as the water flushes the radiator of the compressor unit. You may see a flood of grime and lawn debris as you spray the water through the louvers on the cabinet. Spray all areas inside the cabinet until all debris is flushed away and the water comes out clean.

Next, check the fan motor to see if it needs lubrication. The blower motor may have oiling ports at both ends of the motor shaft. The oiling ports on the motor may be sealed with plastic covers to keep dirt and water out of the motor bearings. Remove the plastic port covers and use an engineer's (flexible-nozzle) oilcan to put a couple of drops of 30-weight motor oil in each port. Replace the plastic covers on the oil ports.

MAINTAINING A WINDOW AIR CONDITIONER

Maintaining a modern window air conditioner is a simple task. As usual, the first step is to consult your owner's manual for specific instructions for maintaining your particular unit.

To gain access to the inside of the unit, check for access panels on the top or sides of the unit. There may be retaining screws that hold the panels: Remove the screws and panels. General advice is to clean the unit periodically to be sure it is free of wind-blown debris and dirt. Clean the condensor fins and inside of the cabinet with the brush attachment on your vacuum cleaner. Next, locate the air filter at the air intake on the front or side of the unit. Some filters simply lift out for cleaning; others are held in place by a filter retainer or panel. Clean or replace the air filter.

One function your air conditioner performs is to remove moisture from the air. This moisture condenses inside the cabinet and runs out through drain holes in the base of the unit. Check for water standing under the fan, or for any musty odor. These symptoms may indicate that a drain hole is clogged. Use a stiff wire, such as a clothes hanger, to reach into the drain holes and unplug them.

Frosting or icing on the air conditioner

If the blower motor requires lubrication, use an engineer's oilcan (flexible-nozzle) to reach into the motor's oil ports.

may be caused by a dirty evaporator or filter, or by an outdoor temperature that is too low. To prevent frosting, clean the evaporator and filter, and do not run the conditioner when the outside temperature is below 70° F (21° C).

After cleaning, turn the air conditioner on and listen for any noises. Look for loose or rattling screws or panels. Check the windows and mounting brackets to see if they are loose and tighten them as necessary. If there is a metallic rattle, check the fan and motor shaft to be sure the fan is tight. If

the fan blades wiggle use a slot screwdriver or hex wrench to tighten the screw on the fan hub. If you hear a whistling noise check for bent evaporator fins. Insert a putty knife between any bent fins and straighten them.

Air Conditioning Checklist

- Clean the air conditioner compressor unit annually.
- Lubricate the fan motor if needed.
- Clean condenser fins and inside the cabinet of a window air conditioner unit periodically.

CHAPTER 5

ELECTRICAL REPAIRS

If you make a mistake when painting or plastering, the problem is only cosmetic and no permanent harm is done. But when a mistake is made in the mechanical trades of electricity and heating the results can be disastrous, and may even harm the house or its occupants. Common sense dictates that the beginner have a healthy respect for electrical and heating repairs, so we will begin our discussion of electrical repairs with the precautionary statement that you alone can determine your experience and capability. If you do not understand what you are doing or why you are doing it, save money by doing other less technically demanding repairs and hire a professional to do electrical repairs. Understand also that insurance companies may not pay for damages caused by faulty workmanship done by a do-it-yourselfer.

The General Electric Company's policy is that the average person can perform all jobs that involve replacement of ordinary electrical devices such as switches, receptacles and light fixtures. The DIYer also can perform such electrical troubleshooting as locating the reason for a doorbell failure and adding an extra outlet. Listed here are the electrical jobs within the abilities of the average reader. If you wish to study the electrical code further, check the National Electrical Code book at your library.

Before beginning electrical repairs turn off the current at the entrance box. Use a circuit tester to be sure there is no current to the device on which you will be working.

Also, if your house has aluminum wiring instead of copper wiring, be sure that any new wiring devices you install — switches, receptacles, lampholders — are marked AL/CU. This marking means the device is approved for installation with either aluminum or copper wiring.

Also, read the preliminary instructions in the following sections on "Understanding Electrical Wire Connections," "Maintaining Polarity," "Using a Circuit Tester," and "Using a Continuity Tester" before turning to any specific repair.

UNDERSTANDING ELECTRICAL WIRE CONNECTIONS

To do electrical repairs the first basic skill to learn is how to connect electrical wires to each other or to electrical devices such as switches or receptacles. Wires that are improperly connected can become loose and can be dangerous. When a wire is loose the electrical current may arc or cause sparks as it jumps from the end of the hot (black) wire to the device screw or to another wire, and the sparks may cause a fire. Or, a loose hot wire can touch the side of the electrical outlet box or wiring device and produce a nasty shock when you touch it. Be sure that all wiring is secured before you cover it.

Connecting Two or More Wires

Use plastic connectors called wire nuts to connect the ends of electrical wires. To make the wire connection, strip the insulation back about ¾ inch on the ends of both (all) wires. Do not twist the ends of the wires together; simply hold the ends of the two wires close together, parallel to each other. Now slip the wire nut over the ends of the two wires and turn the wire nut clockwise until it is tight. Do not over-tighten it or you may break the retaining spring in the wire nut. When the wire nut is tight, pull firmly on each wire to be sure it is secure. If you want to disconnect the wires, use a pair of pliers to pinch the end of the nut and pull the nut off the wires.

Connecting Wires to an Electrical Device

Strip the insulation from the end of the wire, and wrap the end of the wire clock-wise around the wire binding screw. The wire should always be wrapped clockwise so that, as the wire binding screw is tight-ened, the screw will tend to wrap the wire around the screw rather than unwrapping it. To ensure a tight connection, the end of the wire should be wrapped at least three-quarters of the way around the wire bind-ing screw. Be sure to tighten the screw se-curely on the wire.

Did you ever wonder how the pros get such a neat fit of the wire around the wire binding screw? When doing new wiring work try this: Leave several inches of extra wire hanging at the outlet box. Strip the insulation off the end of the wire so that 2 inches of wire is exposed. Wrap the 2 inches of wire around the wire binding screw so that the wire insulation is tight against the screw. Tighten the screw se-curely. Now take the end of the bare wire in your hand and bend the wire back and forth a couple of times. When the wire breaks you will have a neat wrap with no excess wire protruding.

In addition to wire binding screws some electrical devices may have push-in termi-nals or holes for connecting the wires. If you choose to use the push-in terminals, use the wire strip gauge on the receptacle to measure how much insulation should

be removed from the wire end. Just strip off the indicated length of insulation and push the wire end into the proper terminal. Pull gently on the wire to be sure it is se-curely gripped in the terminal.

MAINTAINING POLARITY

Look at a piece of electrical wire (Romex is the brand universally used now). Strip off the plastic insulation and you will see three wires: a black (hot) wire, a white (neutral) wire, and a green or bare (ground) wire.

The *black* wire is the hot wire. It carries the electrical current and should always be connected to other black wires or, on any electrical wiring device, to the *brass* wire binding screw. Always install any electrical switch on the black wire, so that, when the switch is off, there is no power at the outlet or other device.

The *white* wire is the neutral wire. The white wire carries the current back to the service panel. It is grounded at the main service or power panel via a wire connected to the cold water pipe, where the pipe en-ters the house (the pipe must be metal, not plastic). The white or neutral wire should always be connected to other white wires or, on electrical wiring devices, to the *silver* wire binding screw.

The *green* or *bare* wire is the ground wire. The ground wire should be connected only to other ground wires, to the (metal) outlet box, or to the *green* screw on the wiring device.

On flat or appliance cord (wire) you may find that the insulation on one wire is smooth, and on the other wire it is ribbed. The ribbed wire is the white (neutral) wire and it should be attached to the silver screw of the lamp or other device, with the smooth wire attached to the brass screw.

If you examine the plug on a polarized cord you will see that the prong on the white (neutral) side is wider than the prong on the black (hot) side, and the round (ground) prong is on the bottom of the plug. This prong arrangement ensures that

Before working on an electrical outlet, be sure the power is shut off. Check the power with an inexpensive circuit tester. Insert one probe each into the wide and narrow slots of any receptacle. If the tester glows, the power is on.

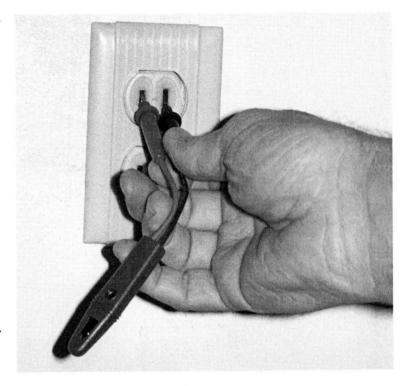

(Below)
To check for ground in a two-slot receptacle insert one probe of the circuit tester into the narrow (hot) slot and touch the other probe to the cover screw. If the screw is grounded, the tester will glow.

serious trouble when making wiring repairs, always turn off the power before working on a circuit, and remember to maintain wiring continuity as you proceed.

USING A CIRCUIT TESTER

For safety, always be sure that the power is turned off when working on an electrical circuit. The safest way to make a power check is to use an inexpensive circuit tester. The circuit tester has a base containing a neon light and two wires with probes that are used to complete an electric circuit. Use a circuit tester to test for power at an electrical switch, outlet, fuse or cord. You can also use the tester to find short circuits, to check circuit polarity, and to test motors or appliances.

To check for power at a receptacle, insert one metal probe into the wide (neutral) slot and the other into the narrow (hot) slot. If the neon bulb on the tester glows there is power at the receptacle, and you must turn off the power at the service panel. If the bulb does not glow the power is off and it is safe to begin work on the receptacle.

when the plug is in the receptacle, *continuity* is preserved. This continuity, in which black (or hot), white (or neutral) and green (or ground) wires always are connected only to like wires, is insurance against damage to any appliance or circuit, or injury to the person in contact with them. To avoid

Test a three-hole receptacle for ground by inserting one probe into the narrow (hot) slot and the other probe into the U-shaped (ground) hole. The tester should glow. The tester should not glow when one probe is inserted into the wide (neutral) slot and the other into the U-shaped (ground) hole.

To check the receptacle for ground, the neon bulb should light when you insert one probe into the narrow (hot) slot and the other into the lower or *U*-shaped (grounding) hole. Now move one probe from the narrow (hot) slot to the wide (neutral) slot, holding the other probe in the *U*-shaped ground hole. The neon bulb should not light when the probes are in this position.

USING A CONTINUITY TESTER

Use a continuity tester to check electrical circuits, cords or switches for continuity, to be sure the unit is intact and working. All continuity tests are done with the power *off*. For the unit shown, the test power is supplied by a pair of AAA batteries. The tester has two probes: One is a nail-shaped probe on the end of the tester body, the second is a small alligator clip connected to the tester body by an electrical wire.

To test continuity in an extension cord, attach the alligator clip to one of the cord prongs. In the photo we are testing the ground. Next, insert the metal probe in the *U*-shaped ground hole in the socket end of the cord. If the tester bulb lights, the ground wire is not broken and is *continuous*. To test the hot and neutral wires in the cord, put the alligator clip on either prong and the probe in the corresponding slot in the plug.

To test a single-pole light switch, turn the switch to the *On* position. Attach the alligator clip to one screw terminal on the switch and touch the metal probe to the other screw terminal. The tester bulb will light if the switch is working.

REPLACING A LIGHT SWITCH

If any light or wall outlet is controlled by a single switch, that switch is called a *single pole switch*. It is easy to replace a single pole switch.

First, turn off the power to that circuit by removing the fuse or switching the circuit breaker at the main service panel. Then use a slot screwdriver to remove the switch cover (wall plate) and the old switch. Loosen the screws on each side of the switch and remove the wires. Then reconnect the wires to the new switch and

A continuity tester has an alligator clip on one end of the wire and a black tube (holds batteries) and probe on the other end. To test an extension cord for continuity, attach the alligator clip to the ground prong at the plug end of the cord and insert the end of the probe into the *U*-shaped (ground) hole in the other end of the cord. If the ground has continuity the bulb in the end of the tube will glow.

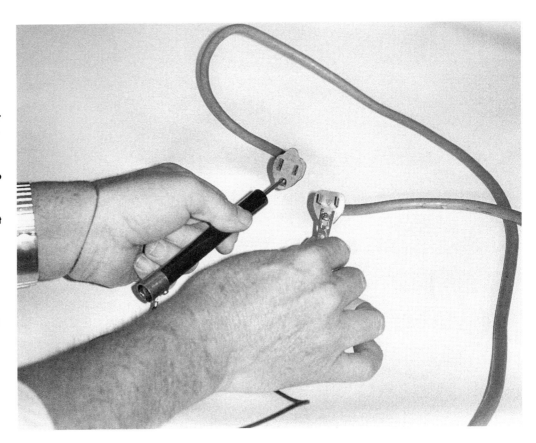

tighten the screws. Or, if the switch has push-in connections, use a bare wire or a small screwdriver blade in the release slot to disconnect the wires. Connect the green (or bare) ground wire to the green screw on the new switch, and replace the switch cover.

Three-Way Switch

If a light or an outlet is controlled from two locations, as at opposite ends of a room or at the top and bottom of the stairs, the switch is a *three-way switch*. Three-way switches are available in the ordinary snap type or mercury type. Remember to specify a three-way switch when buying a replacement. Replacing a three-way switch is slightly different than replacing a single-pole switch, because you have a third, or *common*, wire to work with.

To replace a three-way switch, turn off the power (see page 75) and remove the switch cover. Now look for the common wire: The screw may be a different color—

copper—than the other wire screws, or will be marked *common*. Remove the common wire from the old switch and attach it to the copper, or common, screw on the new switch. You will see a single screw on one side of the new switch: The single screw is the common screw. Then remove the remaining two black wires from the old switch and attach them to the new switch. Attach the green (or ground) wire to the green hex screw on the new switch. If the new switch has no ground screw, attach the ground wire to the metal box or metal switch bracket. Attach the new switch to the box via screws through the mounting strap, and test the switch. If the switch does not work you may have connected the common wire to the wrong screw: Be sure the common wire is connected to the side with a single screw on each of the three-way switches. Inspect the wire connections to be sure all are properly and tightly connected, and try the new switch again.

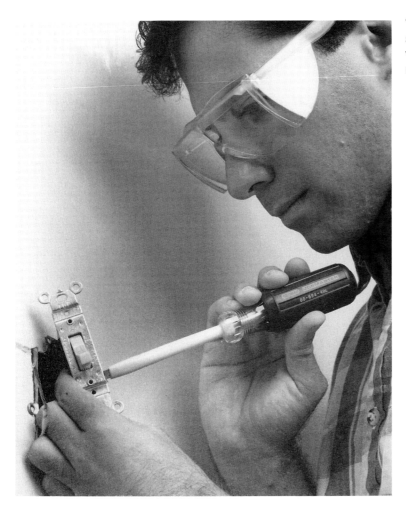

To test an electrical switch, remove the switch from the box and disconnect the wires.

Photo courtesy of Stanley Tool Co.

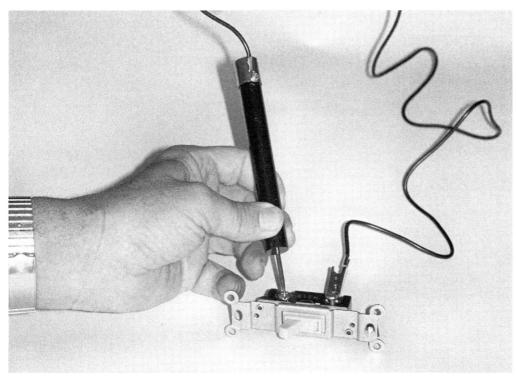

Attach the alligator clip of a continuity tester to one screw on the switch. Touch the probe tip to the other screw and turn the switch on. The tester should glow in the *On* position and should not glow in *Off* position.

Dimmer Switch

Dimmer switches let you control the light level at any light fixture. Dimmer switches extend the life of light bulbs, produce less heat in summer and reduce lighting costs by consuming less power. Use of dimmer switches allows any light to be used as a night-light or a security light. Dimmer switches can be purchased either as single-pole or three-way: Be sure to buy the proper switch for your application. To have dimmer capability at a three-way switch, only one of the two three-way switches can be a dimmer switch: The other switch should be an ordinary three-way switch.

Install the dimmer switches just as you would install any switch—see the instructions on pages 75-76. If the old switch you are replacing has a ground screw, and the box is metal and grounded, attach the ground wire to the outlet box. If the outlet box is plastic, attach the ground wire to the metal bracket on the dimmer switch.

INSTALLING A LIGHT FIXTURE

Most new light fixtures come complete with installation instructions, and will not present any problem for DIY installation. The only exception to this observation might be if you are installing a heavy ceiling fan or an oversize chandelier. If the fixture you are installing is heavier than a normal fixture, be sure the electric box is anchored securely enough to support the heavy fixture. Special brackets are available for hanging heavy fixtures or ceiling fans; look for these brackets at your home center.

When installing a fixture within normal size and weight limits, first shut off the power and remove the old fixture. There may be three wires coming to the old fixture: white, black and green (or bare) wires. As always, observe the color-coding of the wires: Black attaches to black, white attaches to white, and green or ground wire attaches to either the bare wire or to the metal box. Use wire nuts to secure the wires.

REPLACING A RECEPTACLE

As with all wiring devices, receptacles are easy to replace if you follow the principles repeated here. These are: Turn off the power, remove the wall plate, and remove the old device—in this case, a receptacle. Be sure to check the old switch, receptacle or other device and replace it with the same type of device.

Most receptacles will have a pair of black wires on the side with brass screws, two white wires on the side with silver screws, and a ground wire to a green screw on the receptacle or in the metal box. If this describes the receptacle you are replacing, one pair of black-and-white wires brings current to that receptacle, and the other pair of black-and-white wires carries the current on to the next receptacle on that circuit.

After removing the old receptacle, check it to see if there is a metal link between the two outlets, or whether the metal link has been broken. If one outlet is always hot and the other outlet is switched, the link is sometimes broken between the top and bottom outlets. If the link between the outlets on the old receptacle has been broken, use needlenose pliers to break the link between the outlets on the new receptacle. Then attach the wires to the new receptacle exactly as they were attached to the old one. Replace the receptacle and wall plate or cover. Turn the power on and check the receptacle.

Installing GFCI Receptacles

To protect electrical circuits from fire caused by a short circuit or equipment failure, each circuit in your house has a fuse or circuit breaker at the service panel. But fuses and circuit breakers do not react quickly enough to protect humans from dangerous or fatal electrical shock, so the electrical code requires that outlets in dangerous locations be equipped with ground fault circuit interrupters, or GFCIs. GFCIs are most important in any areas where occupants may come in contact with electricity and moisture, which multiplies the shock hazard. Outlets in the kitchen, bathroom and laundry, plus exterior outlets, must be equipped with GFCIs.

How do GFCIs work? In an electrical circuit, the black (hot) wire carries the current to the electrical device, and an equal current returns to the service panel via the white (neutral) wire. The GFCI measures the equal flow of current — both incoming (on the black wire) and returning (on the white wire). However, if a person in contact with the current begins to experience a shock, part of the current goes to ground, so the current drops on the white (or neutral) wire. The GFCI can monitor the difference in current between the black wire and the white wire, and switches off the current. A GFCI will sense a current difference of .005, or five milliamps, and will shut down the current before the person can be injured.

Before working on an electrical circuit, always remember to turn off the power at the service panel. Note also that there are several types of GFCIs available, so be sure to buy the proper GFCI for your application. One type of GFCI has two pairs of black-and-white wires. When installed in the electrical outlet box nearest the service panel (the first outlet on a circuit) it will protect all receptacles on that entire circuit.

ADDING AN OUTLET WITH ON-WALL WIRING

You may need an extra electrical outlet on a wall or ceiling, but have neither the access nor the expertise to thread electric wiring through finished walls or ceilings. Consider using an on-the-wall or surface wiring system, such as one made by Wiremold. A surface wiring system has a variety of plastic base plates and outlet extension boxes to increase the depth of outlet boxes so there is room inside to install added wiring.

To add on-wall wiring, install a baseplate and extension box on any source receptacle, as near as possible to the location

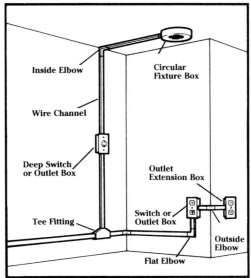

On-wall wiring system.

Courtesy of Wiremold Company.

where you want to install the new receptacle. Then cut the base portion of the plastic wire conduit to the length needed to reach the desired new receptacle location. Use #6 panhead screws to attach the wire channel to the wall or ceiling. At the new receptacle location, screw a baseplate unit to the surface. Run wiring through the wire channel and attach a new receptacle to the wires. Remember always to connect black wires to brass screws, white wires to neutral screws, and green wires to ground screws. Install a box extension on the new baseplate and screw the new receptacle to the extension and baseplate. Finally, install the cover plates on the existing and new outlet boxes. Turn on the power and test the addition with a circuit tester.

REPLACING A LAMPHOLDER

Use pull-chain lampholders to provide a power source or lighting at any location without a switch. The lampholder base may have a single lamp (bulb) socket, or it may include an outlet that will accept a cord plug. The light/plug lampholder is popular for use in a laundry area, so one can also plug in a clothes iron, or in the garage or attic where one might need to plug in a power tool, an extension cord or a trouble light. Using pull-chain lampholders can save money, because they eliminate the need for a wall switch. Lampholders are often used for lighting in unfinished basement, garage, attic or storage space.

With frequent use the pull-chain switch may fail, and you must replace the lampholder with a new one. Turn off the power to the lampholder at the fuse or circuit breaker. Remove the bulb from the socket, then use a slot screwdriver to remove the two screws that secure the lampholder base to the outlet box. Unscrew the assembly ring from the lampholder base to reach the switch mechanism.

There are two terminal screws on the switch mechanism: a black (hot) wire attached to one terminal screw and a white (neutral) wire attached to the other terminal screw. Loosen both terminal screws, and remove the electrical wires from the old switch.

Attach the new switch mechanism to the two wires, and turn the terminal screws tight. Slip the end of the pull chain through the chain hole and position the switch mechanism in the lampholder base. Turn the threaded assembly ring onto the switch mechanism base and tighten it. Now use the two retaining screws to attach the lampholder base to the outlet box. To test the new lampholder turn on the electricity and pull the switch chain.

REMOVING A BROKEN LIGHT BULB

If you break the bulb in a lamp or work light the glass bulb may break flush with the socket. The job now is to remove the broken bulb base from the socket, but there is no bulb to hold onto.

First, disconnect the lamp or work-light cord. If the broken bulb is in a fixed light fixture, turn off the fuse or circuit breaker. Don't touch the open filament on the light bulb until you are sure the power is off. With the power off, use a pair of needle-nose pliers to remove the bulb from the socket. Just slip the tip of the pliers into the socket, grasp the metal rim on the base of the light bulb, and carefully screw it out of the socket. If you don't have needlenose

pliers handy, press the end of a bar of soap into the broken base, being careful not to get cut on the glass. Now twist the bar of soap slowly to unscrew the bulb base from the socket.

REPLACING A DOORBELL BUTTON

Doorbell chimes consist of a button switch at the door(s), a pair of small wires, a transformer that steps the current down from 120 volts to between 10 and 24 volts, and the bell or chime mechanism. Suspect a faulty doorbell button if the system fails to work, because the doorbell button gets the most use and is exposed to the elements.

Remove the button cover at the door to check the doorbell button. Some covers are friction-fit and can simply be pried off the doorbell base. Most covers are held in place by a pair of small screws. To remove the button switch, remove the cover and loosen the two screw terminals connecting the wires to the switch.

To test the circuit, touch the two bare wires together. The bell or chime should sound. If the bell will not sound, use steel wool or fine sandpaper to clean the bare ends of the wires and touch them together again. If the bell sounds, the circuit is intact and the doorbell is the problem.

Buy a new doorbell button at the home center or hardware store. Attach the two bell wires to the two screw terminals and push the bell button. The bell should sound. Install the doorbell cover using the new screws in the button package.

INSTALLING VARIABLE-SPEED CEILING FAN CONTROLS

In the movies of the 1930s and 1940s the only cooling devices in evidence were lazy ceiling fans, devices that became less popular as air conditioning became more common. But with the onset of the energy crisis of the 1970s, ceiling fans came back into fashion. More expensive fans have speed control switches, often on a pull-chain switch. But you can make even the cheap-

Use an emery board to remove corrosion from a yard light socket.

est fan variable speed, and make all fan controls more convenient, by installing a variable-speed switch or control.

Do not use an ordinary light dimmer switch as a fan control switch. It requires a heavier switch to control a fan motor than to control light levels in a lighting fixture. Fan control switches should have at least a 5-amp capacity.

Install the fan control switch just as you would install any replacement switch: power off, like-colored wires joined together with wire nuts.

MAINTAINING EXTERIOR LIGHTING

Exterior lights are exposed to all the elements: Heat, cold and moisture combine to attack and ruin porch and yard lights. A little simple maintenance can go far to keep lights functioning properly.

First, test the light with a circuit tester to be sure no current is present. Unscrew the light bulb and check the socket for dirt and corrosion. Dirt can be blown out with an air compressor or lifted with a portable vacuum unit. If the socket is corroded use an emery board to clean away the corro-

To prevent future corrosion, spray a silicone ignition sealer into the light socket.

Also spray the metal base of the light bulb with the sealer. Replace the light bulb and globe.

Photo by author.

sion, then clean the debris out of the socket.

Spray the inside of the socket with a silicone spray lubricant. This will help weatherproof the socket and will seal it against moisture, as well as ensuring that you can easily remove the light bulb for replacement. Also, spray the metal bulb base and let it dry before replacing the bulb.

Electrical Repairs Checklist

• Turn off the current at the entrance box before starting any electrical repair.

• Learn wiring basics: maintaining polarity, using a circuit tester, using a continuity tester.

• Always observe color-coding of electrical wires.

• Install GFCI receptacles in the kitchen, bathroom and laundry as well as in exterior outlets.

• Maintain exterior lighting to prevent early failure due to the effects of heat, cold and moisture.

CHAPTER 6

HOME SECURITY

I f your home lacks basic security and alarm devices, many dangerous — even deadly — home emergencies can develop. Sophisticated alarm systems are available that can protect you from potential dangers ranging from burglary to house fires, but there are many devices that are inexpensive and easily installed that can provide basic protection from most home hazards. Consider using the following security devices and tests to make your home both safer and healthier.

INSTALLING AND MAINTAINING SMOKE DETECTORS

According to Olin L. Greene of the U.S. Fire Administration, the United States has one of the highest fire death rates in the world. Each year 30,000 people are injured and 5,500 people (including 100 firefighters) die in fires in the United States. To put these figures in perspective, fire kills more people each year than tornadoes, floods, hurricanes and earthquakes combined. The leading cause of residential fire deaths is careless smoking. Those most vulnerable are senior citizens and children under five.

In residential fires, more people die each year from inhaling smoke than from burn injuries. The hazards include not only smoke and fire, but in modern homes plastic materials such as carpeting and upholstery emit toxic fumes when they burn, making today's fires doubly dangerous. Strategically placed smoke alarms can alert

the family and provide precious extra minutes in which to move the family to safety.

Smoke alarms are available in either battery-powered or hard-wired (connected to your house wiring) units. There are reasonable arguments in favor of either type. Some argue that people neglect to replace dead batteries, making battery-powered alarms worthless. Those who favor battery-powered alarms point out that hard-wired alarms will fail to function if electrical wiring is damaged in the fire. My advice is to install at least one battery-powered alarm on each level of the house: in the basement or other furnace/appliance area, where fires frequently originate; in a center hall, near bedrooms where the family sleeps (most

A battery-powered smoke alarm can be installed with a slot screwdriver. Install at least one alarm on each level of the house. Test the battery once a month.

fires occur at night); and in or near the kitchen to warn of cooking fires. Other alarm locations to consider might be attached garages, laundry rooms and workshops.

Make it a point to replace alarm batteries twice a year, on the days when you reset clocks for Daylight Savings Time. Install smoke alarms on the ceiling or on the wall about one foot below the ceiling. The alarms are easy to install — most are held in place by two screws that are supplied with the units — and you need only a screwdriver to make the installation.

To ensure continuous protection, most alarms have test buttons. Push the button once a month to be sure batteries are not dead and the units are operational.

INSTALLING SECURITY ALARMS

Walk out your front door and count down four houses. According to crime statistics, one of those four houses will be burglarized this year. You can pay $2,000 or more to buy a professionally installed home burglar alarm system, but the good news is that the budget-conscious do-it-yourselfer can install his own alarm system for a cost of $200 or even less. The total cost will depend on the type of alarm system you choose, plus the number of options or sensors included.

Hard-Wired Systems

You may want to look into a hard-wired alarm system, such as the Safe House system from Radio Shack. The term *hard-wired* means the alarm is installed and connected directly to a house electrical power circuit, as opposed to being plugged in or battery-powered. Such a system can incorporate magnetic switches, motion detectors, smoke detectors, and most other types of sensors.

Wireless Systems

Another type of DIY alarm is the wireless system. The wireless system relies on radio waves rather than wire communications between the sensors and the control panel. These systems can be installed using only a screwdriver. If a wireless system has the ability to monitor its sensors to ensure that they are performing properly and are communicating with the control panel, it is called a *supervised* wireless. Supervised wireless systems employ computer technology to achieve the self-monitoring features. One example of an inexpensive supervised wireless alarm is the Heath Zenith Model SS-6100. Some of these DIY systems can be connected to a full-time monitoring station.

Self-Contained Systems

Easiest to work with are the self-contained systems. These are like small appliances: They can be plugged into a nearby outlet, or they can be moved as needed. One self-contained system is the Vantage Technology Homewatch 2000, a $150 unit that can be hooked to hard-wired options and/or connected to a full-time monitoring station.

Alarms Checklist

A pro who sells AT&T Security Systems advises that the main feature to look for in an alarm system is not the price but the efficiency of the system. He offers the following checklist when shopping for a burglar alarm:

1. Does the system protect all possible entry points, including all windows and doors?

2. Does the alarm trigger at the point of entry? Some motion alarms sound only after the intruder is inside the home.

3. Is the system prone to costly false alarms, or does it respond only to verifiable break-ins?

4. Who monitors the alarm? Some systems have their own security alarm stations and you are stuck with only that service and trapped by any price increases for the service.

5. How many options are available? Op-

tions should include fire or smoke alarms, freeze alarms for winter vacations, and carbon monoxide and heat alarms.

INSTALLING MOTION DETECTOR LIGHTS

One of the great — and low-cost — security products now available is the motion detector light. These lights are available at home centers at a cost of about $25, including the flood lamps. The motion detector light uses infrared to sense a change in temperature from passing people or cars, and turns on the lights to either welcome friends or warn of trespassers. For example, one common model can sense movement within an arc that is 60 feet long and 60 feet wide.

The motion detector has three adjustments. One, marked *Sens*, is a sensitivity monitor that determines the amount of heat needed to activate the sensor and turn on the light. Some are so sensitive that they can be activated by the intrusion of a small dog or cat. The second adjustment is a built-in photo cell that can be adjusted to permit the lights to be activated at a certain level of darkness (*Daylight*). This prevents activation of the light during full daylight. The third control (*Time*) lets you determine the length of time the light will stay on when triggered. One model, for example, is adjustable from a minimum of fifteen seconds up to eighteen minutes.

To install a motion detector unit first turn off the electrical power at the main fuse or service entry box. Remove the old light fixture; follow the instructions provided with the detector to install it. Remember that wires are color-coded: Use twist-on wire connectors (wire nuts) to connect the fixture wires to the power

Motion detector/ floodlights can detect motion and turn on lights or appliances both inside or outside the house.

Photo courtesy of Stanley Home Automation, Division of The Stanley Works.

wires in the outlet box. Fasten black or red fixture wires to the black (power) wire in the box; fasten the white fixture wire to the white (neutral) box wire, and the green (ground) fixture wire to the green wire in the box. Tug on the wires to be sure they are secured by the wire nuts. Then turn the power on at the service box and test the light to be sure it is working properly. Turn the power off, then fold the electrical wires into the outlet box. Use the new screws to fasten the motion detector to the outlet box, then turn the power on. You'll gain a new sense of security knowing that the motion detector light will alert you to intruders and that you will never again have to approach your house in total darkness.

TESTING FOR HOME HAZARDS

In the past two decades houses have been built much tighter to reduce air infiltration and save energy. As homes are made increasingly tighter and air quality is tested, we have become concerned about the increase in interior air pollution. Many businesses are using scare tactics to exaggerate the problems and to prey upon the concerns of the public. Here is a roundup of common sources of air pollution and the inexpensive testing you can do to monitor your own home air quality.

Carbon Monoxide

Carbon-monoxide poisoning is a common home hazard, especially during the winter heating season. There are 230 *fatal* cases of carbon-monoxide poisoning annually in the United States, plus thousands more cases of poisoning where the victims are sickened but recover. Symptoms of carbon-monoxide poisoning include flu-like symptoms such as drowsiness, nausea, weakness, shortness of breath, red or burning eyes, persistent headaches and fatigue.

What makes carbon monoxide so dangerous is that it is an odorless, tasteless and colorless gas and is therefore very difficult for a person to detect. It is produced by incomplete combustion or poor ventila-

tion of fuel-burning appliances such as oil or gas furnaces, gas cooking appliances, water heaters, fireplaces or wood stoves. Compounding the problem is the fact that, as people act to tighten their houses with caulk and weatherstripping, cooking or heating appliances may not be able to draw sufficient outside air for complete combustion. This may result in a furnace pulling combustion gases back into the house rather than exhausting them safely up the chimney.

In addition to being alert for the physical symptoms mentioned, any or all of which may indicate a health-threatening problem, observe the following checklist to avoid carbon-monoxide poisoning:

• Have your furnace checked and adjusted by a professional to be sure the burner and vent systems are operating properly.

• Check the furnace frequently. Look for yellow flames that indicate an improper gas/air combustion mix, for excessive heat near the furnace, and for rust and scaling in front of the furnace. All these symptoms are signs of poor combustion or venting and should be checked out by a pro.

• While the burner has ignition, hold a lighted match or lighter under the draft hood on the gas water heater. If the match flickers downward or goes out it may indicate dangerous exhaust backflow.

• Any sudden appearance of moisture condensation on windowpanes or under windows may indicate vent or combustion problems and should be checked out by a professional.

There are film-badge sensor cards that turn color when carbon monoxide is detected, but these badges provide testing only for small areas and they do not last long. At this time the Consumer Product Safety Commission (CPSC) and Underwriters Laboratories (UL) have announced their approval of carbon-monoxide (CO) detectors for the home. These detectors are battery-operated, look much like the familiar ceiling-mounted smoke alarms, and emit a loud signal when dangerous levels of

CO are detected. The alarms cost between $50 and $70 each, and contain sensors that must be replaced every three to five years.

Look for carbon-monoxide detectors at home centers. If you do not find the detectors, ask the store manager to order one or more units for you.

Radon

Radon first became an issue when it was detected in houses that were built with materials contaminated by uranium mine wastes. Radon gas may be given off when vegetable matter in the earth decays, and it is suspected of causing as many as one hundred deaths per day from lung cancer. Radon is an odorless, colorless and tasteless radioactive gas, so you must use one or more test devices to determine whether you have a radon hazard in your house.

Radon is measured in *picocuries*. A picocurie is one trillionth of a curie, a unit of measure of radioactivity. The permissible limit for radon is set at 4 picocuries per liter of air, or 4pCi/1. To judge the degree of risk, consider that your lung cancer risk from 4pCi/1 is equivalent to the risk of dying in a home accident; the cancer risk at 20pCi/1 radon exposure is equivalent to the risk of dying in an auto accident.

To test for radon, buy a radon test canister (activated charcoal) at a home center or department store. Open the canister and leave it for three to seven days in your basement or crawl space (or house, if it's built on a concrete slab). Then close and seal the canister and send it off to the laboratory for testing. The cost for the test, including postage and lab work, may be about $20.

Another test is called the alpha track unit. The test uses a sheet of polycarbonate plastic as a recording surface. The exposed plastic sheet is struck by alpha particles from the decaying radon, and is left in place for three to six months. Then a laboratory counts the dents in the plastic to find the level of radon present. This test may cost between $25 and $50. If these low-cost tests show no radon or radon levels under 4pCi/1, your home is safe. If the tests show that radon levels are greater than 4pCi/1, don't panic. Radon levels can often be reduced by inexpensive steps such as caulking cracks in basement floors or walls, sealing concrete walls with waterproofing sealer such as UGL Drylok, or increasing ventilation in the affected area. Check with your local building inspector or Environmental Protection Agency (EPA) office for the name of an approved radon abatement contractor.

Natural Gas

Leaking gas can be hazardous if it is inhaled, deadly if it causes an explosion. If you have a gas furnace or other appliance, be aware of the danger signals of a gas leak.

Natural gas and propane are odorless and colorless. Distributors add chemicals that give the gas its common detectable odor. Check all gas appliances and find out where the gas turnoff valves are located. You'll need to know where the gas valves are in case of emergency.

If you smell gas, observe the following checklist:

- Don't use a match or other flame to check for gas leaks. Check the source of the gas odor: Often it may be a leaking pilot light or gas burner. Turn off the gas to the appliance.

- If the gas odor persists, get the family out of the house. Leave windows and doors open to help dissipate the gas. To avoid any dangerous sparks that might ignite the gas, do not touch light switches or telephones. Go to a neighbor's house to call the gas company service department.

- If you detect any gas smell outside the house it may mean a leaking gas supply line. Leave the area and call the gas company.

- Before doing any digging on your property call your local gas company. They can tell you where the gas lines are located.

- Keep the gas utility company phone number in your emergency number file so you can find it quickly.

Lead Hazards

Lead poisoning has been described as the number one environmental problem facing young children. Exposure to lead can cause permanent brain damage, and young children and pregnant women are especially susceptible. To guard your family against lead poisoning, it is important to observe some precautions.

Lead has now been banned from house paints, but paint made before 1978 contained lead. If your house was built before 1978, leave intact paint alone, because paint removal can create paint chips or airborne dust that may be ingested by occupants. If you must strip the paint in an old house, the law requires that you hire a contractor who is approved by your local EPA office for lead abatement work. Move the family out of the house during the removal process, and be sure the contractor cleans the house with a vacuum specially designed to remove all lead dust.

If you live in older rental housing, ask your landlord to refurbish any peeled paint. Any children in the household may pick up paint chips and eat them, or may breathe in lead dust. Be especially careful to clean and vacuum frequently. Wash down any bare floors or windowsills and trim.

If you live in an older city, the soil in your yard and garden may have a high lead content due to exterior paint erosion over the decades. Have the soil tested for lead before planting any vegetable garden (the vegetables can be contaminated by lead in the soil) or if young children will play on the lawn.

Lead may be present in the solder in water pipes, or in house water faucets, and may be leached out into water you will use for drinking or cooking. Don't soften the water to your cold water supply, where you will normally draw water for drinking or for cooking, because sodium in soft water aggravates lead leaching from pipes or joints. Let faucets run for several minutes to flush out water standing in the pipes

before drinking the water. To find a certified laboratory to test your water for lead, call the local EPA office. Lead tests for water cost about $50.

Old pottery, china, crystal containers or ceramic kitchenware may all contain lead. Do not cook or store food or beverages in suspect containers.

Solder has been banned in U.S. food cans, but you should avoid imported canned food because those cans may still contain solder.

Asbestos

The media's preoccupation with asbestos dangers has been so exaggerated as to warn do-it-yourselfers against doing such minor projects as removing a 9' × 12' linoleum floor. Actually, asbestos came to the attention of the public health authorities when long-term asbestos workers began to develop lung cancer and other respiratory health problems. Most of those afflicted worked for companies that made building products containing asbestos, such as insulation, floor tiles, floorcovering, wallboard taping compounds, pipe insulation and brake drums for cars. The asbestosis and other diseases resulted only after long years of daily or regular exposure to asbestos. Most people will never contact enough asbestos fibers to cause health worries, because asbestos is now banned from use in consumer products.

The potential danger from asbestos is from breathing airborne asbestos particles. In most cases asbestos in the home is in a static condition, not airborne, so there is no cause for worry. Even though your house may contain large amounts of asbestos covering boilers or hot water heating pipes, experts assure us that undamaged asbestos is not a hazard. The Environmental Protection Agency, in their booklet "Report to Congress on Indoor Air Quality," reports a study comparing airborne outdoor asbestos levels with prevailing indoor levels in forty-three federal buildings that contained asbestos materials. The EPA report states: "An interim report . . . indicates no statistical difference between indoor and outdoor levels [of asbestos], even in buildings with damaged asbestos-containing materials."

Wear a dust mask when removing minor quantities of building materials that may contain asbestos fibers, such as ceiling tile. If you are doing a major remodeling job and will be disturbing large amounts of asbestos, check with your local building department, or the local office of the EPA, for the name of a certified asbestos abatement contractor who will remove and dispose of the asbestos materials. As you read this book, look for on-going advice on how to minimize exposure to asbestos and other indoor hazards.

Electromagnetic Force

Environmental concerns now include the possibility that electromagnetic forces may pose a health risk. The sources of these electromagnetic forces may include emissions from any high-power electrical transmission lines that pass near your house and various electrical devices, including electric blankets. While not at this time hoisting a red flag on the subject, the Environmental Protection Agency advises that we practice "prudent avoidance" of long-term exposure to more than 5 milliGauss of electromagnetism. If you have high-power electrical transmission lines near your house, or suspect possible exposure from home electrical devices, you can buy an EMF detector for about $175. The detector is the size of a pocket calculator and measures magnetic fields from 1 to 1,999 milliGauss. If you prefer not to purchase the detector, check the Yellow Pages under "Inspection Service" to find a home inspector who can do the testing for you.

Home Security Checklist

• Replace smoke detector batteries twice each year—at the Daylight Savings Time changes.

• Test smoke detectors once a month.

• Check into home burglar alarm systems: hard-wired, wireless and self-contained.

• Consider installing motion detector lighting on your home's exterior.

• Check for home hazards such as carbon monoxide, radon, natural gas, lead, asbestos and electromagnetic forces.

CHAPTER 7

EXTERIOR

Set up a repair and preventive maintenance schedule for the exterior of your home. Periodic maintenance can prevent small problems from growing into large repairs and ensure that your home always has high curb appeal. If you should ever want to sell your house in a hurry (if, for example, you should get a job transfer), you won't want a long list of neglected repair and maintenance chores that must be done before you can put your house on the market. Periodic maintenance will also help keep everything in working order, preventing such small daily aggravations as sticking locks.

But the best reason for observing a periodic maintenance schedule is that neglecting minor maintenance chores will surely lead to more expensive repairs or the need for total replacement. Siding left unpainted in the short term may ruin the appearance of your house, but leave siding unpainted long enough and the weathering process will cause the siding to split, check and crack. Eventually, the only option available will be expensive siding replacement. For another example, water can enter the cracks in concrete and asphalt (blacktop) drives or walks. If water enters the cracks, freezes and breaks up the slab, you will be left with a rustic cobblestone path where your expensive driveway used to be.

Maintenance chores have a way of expanding to fill up your summer weekends. Consider the future maintenance needed for any particular material you use to build or remodel your home. Do you want to paint (or pay a painter to paint) ordinary wood siding every four to seven years? If you hate painting, you should consider using siding materials that require little or no maintenance. Brick, stucco, aluminum or vinyl (least expensive) siding may offer a low-maintenance choice for those who want to avoid the expense and work of exterior painting. But if you *are* going to paint, choose a quality paint product that will last for years before repainting is needed.

Another trick for making maintenance more tolerable is to plan and schedule your maintenance chores so the jobs—and the expense—don't all fall due at the same time. For example, you don't have to paint your entire house at one time. Instead, you could paint the siding or body of the house one year and paint the house trim the next. This assumes, of course, that you will continue with your present color choices: If you make a new paint color choice for the siding or body of the house you will want to change the trim color at the same time. Fences, decks, storage sheds and detached garages can be painted or stained on off-years, when you don't plan to paint the house.

Try to break your exterior maintenance chores into seasons, when the chores are most timely. Establishing a set schedule for maintenance chores will help you stagger the timing so the chores don't pile up and become an unmanageable burden.

Finally, keep a repair/remodeling diary

to record when the roof was replaced and how often the main sewer needs cleaning. Record the manufacturer's name and color of the paint in each room; include the lot number and pattern of the wallpaper. Keep all warranties and guarantees with the diary, so you can tell at a glance if they are still in effect. When you sell the house, pass the diary along to the new owner. The diary can be a valuable tool to help with future maintenance.

MAINTAINING ROOFING

Inspecting the Roof

Because the great majority of roofs are asphalt shingled, my roof maintenance advice always refers to asphalt roofs, unless otherwise noted. Keep in mind that many of the tips, such as cleaning and inspecting the roof, apply to any roof finish.

Inspect the roof deck in spring after winter storms have passed, and again in fall when summer storms have ended. If you cannot climb you can use a pair of binoculars to inspect the roof from ground level. Check the roof deck for windblown debris such as limbs, twigs or leaves that can trap moisture and interfere with good roof drainage. Check especially in the gaps or races between shingles, where debris can lodge to block water flow from the roof. All debris should be power-washed from the roof deck to ensure that no water or moisture remains on the shingles.

Also inspect the roof flashing. *Flashing* is the metal seal used to waterproof joints where any change or interruption occurs in the roof. Flashing may be either prefinished aluminum or galvanized metal. Aluminum flashing should last the life of the roof shingles, but galvanized metal will lose its zinc coating over time and will require periodic painting to prevent rusting.

Check also for loose, missing or torn shingles. As asphalt shingles age and become brittle from the sun's rays, the shingles dry out and start to lose their protective granules. Check the granules on the shingles, both by visually inspecting the

shingle surfaces and by checking in the rain gutters and under downspouts for signs of excessive granule buildup. Such a buildup is a sign that the shingles are drying out and shedding granules; the roof may soon need replacement.

Make a checklist of each point where repair is needed and save it for reference if you are hiring to have the roof repair done. There are several points to consider when deciding whether you should do roof maintenance and repair yourself or hire professionals. Your age and physical condition, the difficulty of climbing your roof because of its pitch or slope, the height of the roof, and your own supply of ladders or scaffold should all be considered before you try to do roof repair work yourself. Don't forget that renting ladders and scaffold costs money, so you should consider these expenses before figuring out any possible do-it-yourself savings.

The metal flashing seen at valleys, where roof levels change (as between the house and an attached garage) or around gables, dormers or chimneys may need periodic

Do not use house paint to paint galvanized vents or flashing. Thick house paint will peel as metal objects expand and contract, and rust from metal will ruin shingles.

To paint roof vent and flashing, mask the entire shingle area with newspaper and masking tape.

Clean away all peeled paint and repaint vents with an aerosol paint product formulated for metal application.

Replacing the Roof

The useful life of asphalt roofing varies according to the construction of the shingles. Most of the asphalt shingle roofing sold in the past had a maximum expected life of fifteen to twenty-five years. Today, superior construction of the base, where fiber glass has replaced felt, has extended shingle life and warranties to thirty or even thirty-five years. To extend the life of your roof and avoid frequent and costly roof replacement, choose a fiber glass shingle with the longest warranty available.

As stated above, the sun is the enemy of the asphalt shingle. The sun's heat will bake the oils out of the asphalt and leave the shingle brittle; it will cause the dried-out shingles to curl and crack; and it will cause the protective granules to separate from the shingles. All these problems are prime indicators that it is time to replace the shingles.

If you think it is time for a new roof, check the number of shingle layers presently on the roof. Building codes allow you to reroof over one existing layer of shingles, but if the roof has two layers you must strip off the shingles down to the bare wood

maintenance such as painting and sealing with roof mastic. Unpainted galvanized flashing will rust in time, staining the roof and eventually resulting in rust-through and ruin of the flashing. Use a metal primer (buy *rusty-metal primer* if rust has already started) and a metal paint topcoat such as DeRusto, Galva-Grip, or other paint formulated specifically for use on metal.

roof sheathing and start fresh.

Note that the reroofing period is the ideal time to correct any other roof problems. At this time you can install extra vents or convert the roof ventilation system to continuous ridge/soffit venting. Better ventilation will cure other roof and attic problems: Roof ice dams are caused by buildup of attic heat, and high attic temperatures in summer contribute to early failure of the shingles.

Tearing the old roofing off also provides an opportunity to inspect the roof sheathing, soffits, fascia (a board covering the joint between the top of a wall and the projecting eaves) and trim for rot or water damage, and to repair or replace damaged boards. In cold climates, where ice dams are common, this is also a good time to install a wide roof membrane at the edge of the roof to prevent water backup and roof leaks, and subsequent water damage to the house interior. Your roofing dealer can help you assemble all the materials needed.

Correcting Roof Ice Dams

The term *roof ice dams* describes ice buildup at the eaves or overhang of a roof. Because water from rain or melting snow can run down the roof and form pools behind these ice dams, the water may actually run backward up the roof and under the shingles, entering the house and causing expensive damage to the plaster or wallboard walls or ceilings of the house interior. To guard against the entry of dammed-up water under the shingles, roofers in cold climates install a 5- to 6-foot-wide barrier or membrane under the shingles at the edge of the eaves.

Roof ice dams can occur in any area where there is winter snow, freezing temperatures, and prolonged periods of cold weather combined with a lack of sunshine to melt the snow and clear the roof. In the winter of 1978-1979, for example, roof ice dams were a problem from Minnesota to Texas, because snowfall was widespread

and cold, cloudy weather was prolonged.

Roof ice dams occur because of heat buildup in the attic. This attic heat buildup is caused by too little attic insulation, which allows furnace heat to pass through the ceilings and insulation and raise the attic temperatures. When that attic air is heated it cannot escape unless there is adequate roof/attic ventilation. When snow lays on the roof the heat trapped in the attic melts the snow from the underside, or shingle side, of the roof. (If nature — the sun — provided the meltdown, the snow would melt from the top down and run harmlessly off the roof.) Now the melted snow runs down the warm roof to the colder eaves, where there is no heat buildup on the underside. When the melted snow meets this cold soffit or roof overhang area it refreezes, forming ice dams.

The cure for roof ice dams is twofold: First, upgrade the attic insulation to prevent house heat from escaping into the attic, then increase attic ventilation so any heat that escapes into the attic can be exhausted to the outdoors. The best attic ventilation system is the continuous ridge/soffit vent system, and such a system can be retrofitted on your roof. This is best

Snow melted from the upper roof runs down and refreezes at the roof edge, forming ice dams. Note the sagging gutters and water running past ice-clogged gutters and down the house siding.

If you live in snow country buy a long-handled snow scraper to remove the snow from the roof edges and reduce ice buildup. Professional roofers can use steam devices to remove ice dams and end water backup.

done when you are reroofing. Such a system is referred to as a *Cold Roof System*, and if the roof/attic is properly built and ventilated you will have no roof ice dams.

Two precautions are necessary here. First, you can buy electrical heating cable to melt the ice at the eaves to prevent the formation of roof ice dams. These heating cables are a very poor substitute for proper insulation and ventilation. A properly built ventilation system requires no energy to operate, as the heating cables do. Second, there are those who now propose that attics can be built without having — or needing — ventilation. This may be true, assuming that at the time of initial construction one can install a vapor barrier so efficient that no moisture can possibly enter the attic. But for existing houses with little or no vapor barrier built into the ceilings, attic heat/moisture buildup can pose real problems, and ventilation should be maintained.

Maintaining Turbine Ventilators

Turbine ventilators became popular during the early days of the energy crisis. Turbine vents can augment the attic ventilation to provide a cold roof deck and help reduce both air-conditioning loads and roof ice dams in winter. Unfortunately, many people neglect the hard-working turbines and the bearings may soon fail, making turbine replacement necessary.

The good news is that if turbine bearings fail, you can easily remove the old turbine and replace it with a new one. Take a can of aerosol lubricant on your next roof inspection; it's easy to lubricate the bearings and extend the life of the turbine vent. The only tool you will need is a slot screwdriver to remove the sheet metal screws that secure the turbine to the base. Remove the screws, lift up and lubricate the turbine, and replace the turbine on the base.

MAINTAINING GUTTERS

Rain gutters used to be considered an essential part of a house. In the building boom that followed World War II, when houses were built with wider overhangs or eaves, many builders began to eliminate rain gutters in the belief that the wider eaves would drop the water farther from the house foundation. Depositing the water farther from the foundation would en-

Adding turbine vents can help prevent roof ice dams and remove summer heat from the attic. Use a screwdriver to remove the turbine from its base.

Use an aerosol lubricant to oil the shaft and bearings of the turbine vent.

To ensure good roof drainage, clean the rain gutters each fall. A gutter cleaning kit attached to a wet/ dry vac lets you clean gutters from ground level.

Photo courtesy Sears.

sure that roof water would run away and eliminate wet basements. This assumption was in some cases true, and many such houses have no drainage problems in spite of the fact that they have no roof gutter systems. On some houses, however, the decision not to install rain gutters proved to be bad judgment; many houses without rain gutters have wet basements or other drainage problems. The owners of the homes, seeing that the builder decided against installing gutters, assumed that the builder was right, even though the evidence — the wet basements — indicated that the houses should have gutters. I have inspected houses to find a cure for a wet

basement, only to find that the problem could be cured with rain gutters. "But," the owner protests, "the builder didn't install rain gutters, so why should I?" The answer is: Because you have a wet basement.

If you have water entry problems and do not have rain gutters, have a gutter system installed. Rain gutters collect all the water — rain or melted snow — from the roof, divert the water to various downspouts, through ground pipes or splash blocks, and deliver the water far enough away from the house so that the water can't run back to the foundation and cause a wet foundation or wet basement.

Metal gutters will peel if they are painted with thick house paint. Use a heat gun to remove peeling paint, then recoat with a metal paint product.

Maintenance of rain gutters includes cleaning the gutters periodically to remove any dirt, leaves, twigs or other debris that could block the gutters and prevent water from flowing freely through them. If the gutters are aluminum or plastic they will need no painting. If you have galvanized steel rain gutters they must be painted. One common cause of peeled paint on galvanized gutters is using too-thick paint, such as full-bodied house paint, to paint the metal gutters. The metal expands and contracts with changes in the temperature, and this expansion/contraction causes the heavy paint film to peel. If you have peeled paint on galvanized gutters you must remove the failing paint down to bare metal, then redo the gutters with a paint formulated for use on metal. If you insist on using ordinary house paint on metal gutters, thin it to the maximum to ensure that you leave a very thin protective paint film on the metal.

Be sure the gutters are tightly connected to the house, not loose or sagging. Check the horizontal rain gutters with a level each spring to be sure there is a slight slope to the gutter downspouts, so water cannot stand in the gutters. Ice that forms on the

gutters in winter may pull the gutters away from the house, so spring is the best time to check for damage.

To secure gutter sections, drill a ⅛-inch hole in the gutters.

TRIMMING TREES

Trees can help shelter the house from storms and can moderate temperature extremes while adding beauty and value to the property. For these reasons arborists

Use pop-type rivets to secure gutter sections together. To disassemble gutter sections, use a ⅛-inch bit to drill out the rivet.

often marvel at the fact that homeowners carefully tend their lawns while totally neglecting trees. Trimming trees requires specialized knowledge, so for most people it is not a DIY task. It requires some expertise to know which limbs to trim and how to trim the tree so that balance and symmetry are maintained. But whether you do your own trimming or have it done by pros, you should be aware of the need to keep trees properly trimmed.

A young tree should be trimmed to direct the shape and direction in which it will grow. Eliminating a weak fork in the tree can protect the tree from future wind damage and splitting at the fork. Any major fork that grows at an angle of more than 30 degrees can be weak and prone to wind damage or splitting.

As a tree grows it may develop suckers, and some limbs may die. This deadwood can provide the entry point for disease, or the deadwood can split into live wood and damage the tree if it becomes wind-blown. All deadwood should be trimmed out of the tree. You should not trim without consulting a local tree expert. For example, in some areas oak trees that are trimmed or

pruned in late spring are prone to attack by oak wilt. Trimming elm trees during the growing season between April and October can invite Dutch elm disease.

If grass will not grow under your tree, trim and thin the crown of the tree to let sunlight penetrate the canopy. If the crown of the tree overhangs the house roof or shades the siding, the roofing and siding may not dry out after a rain, and this can cause growth of mildew or dry rot. Thin out the crown of the tree to prevent moisture damage to the roof and siding. The thinned tree crown will also let wind pass through more easily, reducing the wind load and the possibility of wind damage to the tree.

If you have a weak fork in a tree an expert can cable the tree, tying the forks together with aircraft cable to prevent weak forks from becoming wind-blown.

Second only to disease, lightning damage is a major cause of tree loss. Experts can assess the tree's value and consider whether or not to install lightning equipment. If the tree is closer than 10 feet to the house, lightning can also strike a tree and "sideflash" to hit the house. Look in the Yellow Pages under "Lightning Protection Equipment" to find an expert.

CORRECTING A WET BASEMENT

Wet basements are an *exterior* problem, because the National Association of Home Builders (NAHB) estimates that 95 percent of all wet basement problems are the result of rain or melted snow pooling around the house foundation and running into the basement. You may read texts that blame high water tables for the wet basements, but the water table is very rarely the cause. The water table is the level at which the earth is continuously wet, and does not encompass surface water. If the water table is deep enough, you can build a basement with confidence that there will be no moisture problems from the water table, and that any problems that develop are the result of surface water running into the basement.

If you are unconvinced that your wet basement is the result of surface water from outside running into the basement, there are several ways you can check the water source. First, ask your building inspector

To perform proper tree pruning, pros use ropes, harnesses and truck-mounted hydraulic "cherry picker" lifts. For safety's sake, leave this job to those who have the proper equipment.

A dry basement begins at the rain gutters. Clean and inspect gutters in spring and fall to ensure that they will deliver roof water away from the house foundation.

the depth of the water table in your area. If he indicates there is no problem with a high water table, your problem is probably caused by surface water. Next, query your neighbors on all sides of the house to find if they have basement water problems, too. It is very unusual for the water table to be a problem in one house, when all the basements around it are dry.

If your house is the only one in your area with a basement water problem, put on a raincoat and go outside *during* — not after — a brisk-to-heavy rainfall. Inspect the route water takes on your property. Do rain gutters pick up roof water and deliver it to the ground via ground pipes that are at least 8 feet long? Water that is deposited or pooled close to the foundation can soak back through the soil and wet the foundation wall. Check along all horizontal gutters to be sure water is not overflowing the gutters and dropping where you do not want it. If you see signs of water overflow-

ing the gutters you should be able to figure out what the problem is: clogged gutters, too-small gutters or damaged gutters. Depending on the problem, clean the gutters, replace them with larger ones that have greater capacity, or have sagging gutters re-attached so water cannot overflow.

The next step to solving basement water problems is to check around the perimeter of the foundation for pools of water. If water is permitted to collect or pool within 5 feet or less from the foundation it can seep back and wet the basement wall. Mark these low spots where water pools and fill them with topsoil to level them, so water will run away from the foundation rather than pooling and soaking there.

One area where water collection and/or absorption is a common problem is in flower gardens or plantings next to the foundation. Any water that falls into these planting areas, where the soil is purposely kept loose for cultivation, will soak down

An inspection of the house exterior may reveal a downspout with no ground pipe, so water is delivered alongside the foundation wall. A crack between the sidewalk and the foundation wall invites water entry into the basement.

and cause a basement water problem. It is best to avoid foundation plantings where you have a basement water problem.

In one recent case a basement water problem was solved with $65 worth of black dirt (4 cubic yards). To do this we used masking tape to fasten a 2-foot carpenter's level to a 10-foot length of gutter downspout pipe. With the downspout pipe set perpendicular to the foundation, we put one end of the downspout against the foundation. We then checked the slope or grade of the lawn away from the foundation. We worked to achieve at least 5 inches of slope in the 10 feet of run, or ½-inch slope per running foot. This is enough slope to ensure that water will run quickly away from the foundation, and will run at least 10 feet away before any pools can form.

One common — and very poor — piece of advice to homeowners is to be sure that any sidewalks, patios or driveways placed adjacent to the house be level. Any hard surface slab such as concrete will catch a good deal of water, and if the slab is level or tilts slightly toward the foundation, all the water (rain or snowmelt) that falls on

the slab will be delivered against the foundation and from there into the basement. If you are planning a patio or drive adjacent to or near the foundation, be sure to build concrete forms so that the finished slab will slope away from the foundation.

The first steps to relieve basement water problems are those previously listed: Install and maintain a proper gutter system

Inexpensive fiber glass splash blocks can help divert water away from the foundation.

Use a nylon brush to apply the etching solution to the efflorescence. On very stubborn stains use a stiff scrub brush.

Photo courtesy UGL.

Inside the basement, mix etching crystals with water to clean efflorescence from the concrete wall. Note telltale water stains on walls.

Photo courtesy UGL.

to collect roof water and direct it away from the foundation, then correct the grade around the foundation so the water will be directed and deposited at a distance from the foundation. If this seems beyond your do-it-yourself capabilities, call in a landscape contractor to do the job of establishing a proper grade. The last step is one that people often try as a first remedy: Fill all cracks in the basement walls with patching/hydraulic cement, let the patches dry, then apply a basement waterproofing coating such as UGL's Drylok over the entire surface of all basement walls. One simple fact cannot be emphasized too strongly:

Masonry paints and coatings usually will fail if water stands against the exterior side of a basement wall. The easiest, cheapest and most effective way to dry up a wet basement is to set up a system of roof gutters and lawn grading to keep the water away from the wall. Remember, if you have water coming through a crack in a basement wall, the crack is not the problem: The water is the problem, and diverting the water away from the wall, not patching the crack, is the solution.

Roofing, Gutters and Basement Checklist

• Inspect the roof deck and flashing in spring and fall for repairs.

• When planning a reroofing job, correct any other roof problems at the same time.

Install extra vents, inspect for rot and water damage, and install a roof membrane if ice dams are a problem.

- Upgrade attic insulation as the first step toward correcting ice damming.
- Clean and lubricate turbine ventilators.
- Clean gutters, check downspout slope, add splash blocks if necessary to divert roof water away from the house.

MAINTAINING AND REPAIRING SIDING

The term *siding* once referred to wood, stucco or brick exterior cladding. Today modern siding materials include steel, aluminum and vinyl siding. Although there are separate maintenance steps for each of these materials, all must be cleaned period-ically to ensure the appearance and to protect the finish. For example, we hear much about air pollution in relation to personal health risks, but that same air pollution can also damage or stain the finish on exterior siding.

All types of siding must be kept clean, both to maintain appearance and to extend life. No matter which type of siding you have, buy or rent a pressure washer, one capable of producing 500-pounds-per-inch of pressure, and clean the house siding each spring. An annual spring cleaning will remove dirt and accumulated grime as well as removing potentially corrosive airborne chemicals. Often, a siding finish that looks dull and aged may simply need cleaning, and the cleaning will save you the work

Apply a high-quality concrete sealer to the entire concrete wall. Experts recommend that you use two coats of sealer on the lower sections of the wall as an extra barrier in the stained areas.

Photo courtesy UGL.

and expense of a paint job. Even if you must paint, the first step should be a thorough cleaning of the siding. A cleaner for each type of siding is suggested below, but you can find an appropriate cleaner for any of the siding or building materials at most janitorial supply houses. Look in the Yellow Pages under "Janitorial Equipment and Supplies" to find the right cleaner for any material.

Wood Siding

An old reliable cleaner for painted wood siding is trisodium phosphate, or TSP, a dry powder cleaner available at most paint supply houses and home centers. Depending on the mixing proportions of TSP and water, TSP can be a heavy-duty cleaner or can even be used as a deglosser for high-gloss paints. If you live in an area where phosphates are banned, products that are labeled TSP but are phosphate-free cleaners are available. One such product is Savogran TSP-PF (Phosphate Free).

If the house is stained by mildew, mix ordinary chlorine bleach in a 50-50 solution with water. Wet the siding with a garden hose and nozzle, then use a garden sprayer or a pressure sprayer to apply the bleach solution to the siding. Let the chlorine bleach work on the dirt and mildew, lifting it from the surface. Then pressure-wash the siding to remove all residue and clean the siding.

One note: Many people may be concerned whether the 50-50 chlorine bleach/water solution might be dangerous to grass or flowers. As a precaution to protect the plants, cover any foundation plantings with plastic, and flush away the solution with lots of water after cleaning.

Unpainted Wood Siding

Hundreds of thousands of houses built in the 1960s and later have natural cedar or redwood siding that was left unpainted on the premise that it would "weather to a lovely natural gray." The problem is that the promised gray color is nothing more

than dirt and mildew, and in most cases the graying is not uniform but is splotchy and uneven. To restore the unfinished wood to a new-wood look, follow the directions given above for painted wood siding. Wet the wood, apply a 50-50 solution of water and chlorine bleach, and power-wash the dirt away. An option, though possibly more expensive than using bleach, is to use one of the wood deck cleaners such as Dekswood to clean the siding. You will be amazed to see the bare wood turn to a fresh-sawn wood tone. When the wood has dried completely, apply a clear wood sealer, a clear wood water repellent with mildewcide, or a pigmented stain with ultraviolet sun blocker.

Aluminum Siding

If aluminum siding is dull and faded, clean the oxidized paint away with a deck cleaner. Follow the label directions for cleaning aluminum or fiber glass. After cleaning the siding and letting it dry, check the appearance. If the paint is still dulled, use a clean white cloth to apply a clear coating product such as Penetrol to the aluminum siding. This will restore the paint finish to its original luster. When it is time to repaint, such a product will also provide an excellent base.

For painting aluminum siding use a premium acrylic latex house paint. Most manufacturers recommend their top quality acrylic latex as the proper choice for painting aluminum siding. Check the paint label to make sure the paint is recommended for aluminum application.

Vinyl Siding

Today, 80 percent of replacement siding sold is vinyl. Vinyl has the same warranty as steel or aluminum siding, but costs less. Prices may vary regionally; average prices put vinyl siding costs at about $3 per square foot and aluminum or steel siding at between $5 and $6 per square foot.

Experts suggest that you should never paint vinyl siding. Because the color of vinyl siding extends through the product, and does not sit on the surface as a protective coating, vinyl siding should be cleaned, not repainted. To clean vinyl siding, mix ⅓ cup of laundry detergent with ⅔ cup of TSP (trisodium phosphate) in a gallon of water. Wet the vinyl siding with clear water from the garden hose, apply the detergent/TSP/water mix with a soft scrub brush, and then rinse again with water from the hose. For removing tough stains on vinyl or aluminum siding, try GOJO, a hand-cleaning product available at most auto repair stores. Clean the stains with the product and rinse the siding with clear water.

Repairing Damaged Lap Siding

Lap siding is a term used to describe any siding material that is installed in horizontal rows, with each succeeding row of siding overlapping the previous row. Thus lap siding applied in horizontal rows includes wood, aluminum, steel and vinyl.

Some repair texts instruct the DIYer to cut out a damaged section of siding and insert a patch in its place. This is very poor advice. If you examine your siding you will see that it was installed with a concern for the finished appearance. This means that there are a minimum of end joints, and these siding end joints occur in a random pattern. Perform all repairs in a workmanlike manner so that there are no obvious patches on the exterior siding.

If a piece of siding is damaged, remove and replace the entire piece so no extra end joints are made. For wood siding, the replacement means using a thin prybar to carefully pry off any end caps, then prying upwards at each nail to loosen and remove the siding piece. After you have removed the damaged siding piece, replace it with a piece of siding that is an exact match, and prime and paint so it will match your existing siding.

Prefinished siding such as aluminum, steel or vinyl has no visible nails. The siding is held in place via interlocking edges on the panels, or is *blind nailed* — nailed so no nail heads are visible. Vinyl siding must be able to expand, so make sure it's not nailed tight. Because removing and replacing this siding is difficult, you should have repairs to aluminum, steel or vinyl siding done by a professional.

Renewing Stucco

Stucco consists of a base coat of Portland cement that is washed with a second coat of white or colored cement, and finally *dashed*, or textured, with a patterned top finish. This top finish is a cementitous coating and may be the same color as the wash coat or a complementary color.

Stucco is so durable that it may be renewed for many years, even decades, by a simple power washing. Check the Yellow Pages under "Janitorial Equipment and Supplies" to find a dealer who can recommend a good masonry cleaner. To clean stucco, just follow the same procedure outlined for cleaning wood or aluminum siding. Pre-wet the stucco with a fine mist of water and let it set a few minutes to loosen dirt and grime. Then apply the masonry cleaner per the manufacturer's instructions. Let the cleaner set on the stucco surface for five to ten minutes so it can lift the grime. Then power-wash the dirt and grime away. If the stucco appears to be dirty you may have to repeat the process to remove decades-old accumulated grime.

Stucco is a masonry finish, and is not intended to be painted, especially in cold climates where moisture transfer from indoors to outdoors is a problem. If you intend to paint stucco, check with masonry contractors in your area to find out how well painted stucco stands up in your particular climate. If you decide to paint the stucco, be sure to use a quality acrylic emulsion paint such as Thorosheen, available at most masonry dealers. Check the Yellow Pages under "Stucco and Textured Coating Contractors" for a masonry supply dealer.

Stucco Repair and Refinishing

Stucco is a cement material. It is applied with a textured finish, and repairs are usually needed only after the finish stucco has aged for some period. It is difficult to patch a hole or crack in stucco so that the patch material matches the existing stucco either in color or in texture. The only thing that looks worse than damaged stucco is badly patched stucco, with the patched areas standing out like stripes on a zebra. Drive through an area of stucco homes and check the mess made when insulation was blown into exterior walls through holes drilled in the stucco and then the holes were patched over. Some home repairs cannot be successfully done by amateurs, and patching stucco is one. In most cases any possible savings from doing one's own patching of stucco is far outweighed by the loss in resale value of the house due to the unsightly repairs.

While patching random holes or cracks in stucco is difficult to do, redashing the stucco can be done by a handyman. This is because on a redash job the stucco will cover the entire exterior, so there is no mismatched texture pattern or color. When stucco needs to be refinished, the best solution is to redash the stucco, meaning to respray the cement/stucco finish to renew the appearance. You can also apply a new masonry finish with a stiff brush, or you can rent a hopper-type sprayer that can spray the cement finish over the old stucco. Check the Yellow Pages for a dealer who works with cement/stucco finish products.

Log Siding

Because of their size, logs may experience high shrinkage as the house settles or loses moisture. Because of this high shrinkage you should never use paint or varnish on log exteriors. Both materials leave a brittle protective film on the surface that may crack or check as the logs shrink and settle.

Follow this three-step procedure, recommended by the National Association of Home Builders, for proper maintenance of log houses:

1. Dissolve four ounces of Savogran TSP-PF (phosphate-free) or low-phosphate detergent in a solution of one quart of chlorine bleach and three quarts of water to make a gallon of cleaning solution for log houses. One gallon of this cleaner will clean approximately 250 square feet of log siding. (This formula can also be used to clean any wood siding.) Use this procedure to clean either older or new log homes to remove grime, mildew or air pollutants. Spray the log siding to wet it, then use a garden sprayer to spray the cleaner on the logs. Let the solution soak for fifteen to thirty minutes, or until the grime begins to lift. Use a power washer of not more than 500-pounds-per-square-foot pressure to wash the cleaner and grime away.

2. After cleaning the logs, apply one or two coats of a wood preservative such as Wolman Clear, Flood Seasonite or Sikkens Wood Preservative.

3. To preserve the natural wood color use a transparent wood treatment such as Flood CWF (for "clear wood finish"), Wolman Raincoat or Weatherall Log Guard. To add color without covering the wood grain use Olympic Semitransparent Stain, pigmented Wood Guard, pigmented Log Guard, or Wolman Raincoat with Natural Wood Toner.

Siding Checklist

• Clean wood siding with trisodium phosphate solution; clean mildew stains with chlorine bleach solution.

• Power-wash unpainted wood siding with a chlorine bleach solution to give a new-wood look.

• Clean oxidized paint on aluminum siding with deck cleaner.

• Wash vinyl siding with a detergent/TSP/water solution.

• Power-wash stucco to lift grime.

• Consider redashing stucco that appears to need refinishing or repainting.

MAINTAINING WINDOW AND DOOR TRIM

The use of vapor barriers in exterior wall construction has greatly reduced the problem of paint peeling on siding. In older houses built before vapor barriers were available, you can prime the interior surface of exterior walls with alkyd (oil-base) primer. This will provide a good seal on the walls and will slow or stop the migration of interior moisture through the exterior wall, where it peels the paint on the siding. Peeling of paint on exterior window and door trim is still a problem, however. Often, especially on houses that have brick or stucco exteriors, the gap around the windows provides the path of least resistance for interior moisture passing outward through the walls. Because the moisture cannot easily pass through mortar, it will instead pass through the trim around openings (windows and doors), peeling the paint.

This peeling on trim is also seen on modern houses that have vapor barriers in the walls. In order to cut openings in exterior walls and install window and door components, the carpenters must cut a hole in the plastic vapor barrier. This opening again provides the path of least resistance for any moisture moving from the house interior to the outside.

When building or remodeling, use window and door packages that have pre-primed wood-, aluminum- or vinyl-clad trim to greatly reduce or eliminate the problem of peeling paint on window or door trim. For existing trim that will not hold paint well, there are several precautions you can take when repainting to reduce peeling paint.

If you have peeling trim paint, first remove all the existing paint down to bare wood, using a scraper or heat gun. You must completely remove the old paint, because any paint left on the surface and painted over will most likely lift and peel later, ruining your new paint job.

To reduce future paint peeling there are two options. First, use latex trim paint on the problem areas. Latex paint film *breathes* (lets moisture pass through more readily than a film of alkyd paint), so it resists peeling better. Or, for better paint adhesion, first apply one or more coats of a paint conditioner such as Penetrol to the bare wood. Apply repeated coats of the conditioner until the wood trim is well saturated with the material. Then mix alkyd paint and paint conditioner as directed on the conditioner label, usually one pint of conditioner per gallon of alkyd paint. Apply the thinned paint over the dried paint conditioner, using two coats.

Replacing Window Screens

Replacing the wire on wooden window screens is a simple task. Buy aluminum or fiber glass screen wire in a size large enough so that the new wire overlaps the screen opening. Remove the old screen molding by prying upward with a small chisel or prybar. Remove the damaged screen. Place the new screen fabric so it overlaps the screen opening. Stretch the screen fabric both for length and width and staple it in place. Replace the screen moldings. Use a utility knife to cut away the excess screen.

To replace the screen in an aluminum window or doorframe you will need a tool called a *spline roller*. The spline roller is a small hand tool with a roller on each end. One roller has a convex edge: Use this roller to roll the screen fabric into the groove in the frame. The other roller has a concave edge: Use this to force the spline into the window frame groove atop the screen fabric.

Use a sharp knife or awl to lift one end of the old spline out of the screen frame, and pull out the spline and screen fabric. Do not try to cut the new screen fabric to fit before installing it: Let it overlap the screen frame by a couple of inches on each side.

If the new fabric is metal, use the convex roller edge to form a groove in the screen

Use the convex wheel on a roller tool to shape screen wire into the groove in the frame.

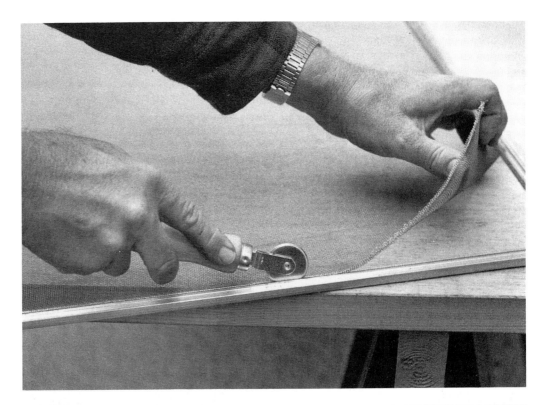

After shaping the wire into the groove, use the concave wheel on the roller tool to compress the vinyl spline and force it into the retaining groove.

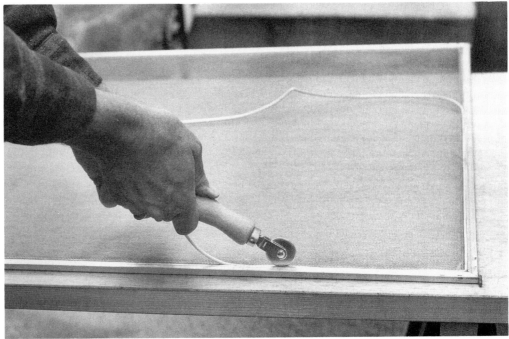

fabric, then force the new spline into the groove in the metal fabric. If you are installing fiber glass fabric use only the concave roller wheel to form the groove and to press the spline into the groove. When you have finished, use a razor knife to cut away the excess screen fabric.

Replacing Window Glass

Replacing window glass in a wooden frame is a straightforward repair. Always wear heavy leather gloves when working with broken glass.

If you have broken glass in a metal window frame, you may have to take the frame

apart to install new glass. If you are not sure of your ability here take the metal window frame to a local hardware store for glass replacement.

To replace glass in a wooden frame, first remove the broken glass. To do this you must remove the old window glazing compound or putty. Heat the putty with a propane torch or a heat gun. This will soften it and make it easier to remove. Use a putty knife to remove the old putty after it is softened. When you have removed the old putty you will see small metal triangles, called *glazing points*, that hold the glass in the groove against the frame. Use needle-nosed pliers to remove the old glazing points. Use sandpaper and a scraper to clean out the groove.

Now measure the glass for both width and length. Take the exact dimension, measuring tight to the frame. The glass cutter will subtract ¼-inch off each dimension so the glass will slip into the frame and will not break when the wood frame expands and contracts.

Lay a thin bed of putty into the frame to seal the glass on the inside of the frame. Lay the new glass into the frame and press it gently down so the putty oozes out on the inside of the frame. Now drive new metal glazing points into the frame to secure the glass.

When the glazing points are in place, roll a bead of latex glazing compound into a rope and press it where glass and window frame meet. Then use a putty knife to form the glazing compound into a 45-degree curb between the glass and the frame. (Latex glazing compound is also available in caulk tubes.) Let it dry, then apply a coat of primer and paint the window frame. When you paint, let the paint overlap onto the glass so it forms a shield against moisture entry between the glass and the wooden frame.

Use a power-washer to clean oil drips and other grime off the asphalt driveway. Power-washers can be rented for about $35 per half-day.

Prefill very wide or deep cracks with clean sand; use a brush to sweep away excess sand.

SEALING AND REPAIRING THE DRIVEWAY

Asphalt or blacktop is often used to pave residential driveways. Asphalt is a bituminous material, a resinous hydrocarbon found in petroleum. It is inexpensive, easy to place, and can be picked up and reprocessed to be laid again, so it can be competitive with concrete as a paving material. But, like concrete, durability does not mean that it requires no maintenance. Any slab, whether concrete or asphalt, will expand and contract with changes in the weather, and this expansion/contraction cycle will produce cracks in the slab. Once cracks develop, water can enter and freeze and expand in cold weather, further cracking the slab. Water that penetrates cracks can also wash away the gravel base under the slab, and the weight of cars can break holes in the slab where base support has been washed away. Water that runs along the slab edges can undercut the gravel base at the edges, and passing cars will break off these edges and damage the slab. As a result your expensive driveway will be reduced to a rustic cobblestone path.

The key to extending the life of the driveway is routine maintenance. In the past, patching cracks in asphalt or concrete slabs was a messy process of mixing a patch material and troweling it into the cracks. With luck, the crack would not re-open before you got the trowel cleaned. Today, tube-type caulk products are available that reduce crack patching to a simple clean-and-caulk procedure. To clean the cracks use a masonry chisel to pry out any loose chips. Dirt can be removed with a power-washer or by using the nozzle of the garden hose. When using a petroleum-based patcher on asphalt you must let the cracks dry completely before applying the caulk/patcher. Latex based concrete patchers can be applied to a still-wet crack.

Also available is a peel-and-stick "bandage" or patch for asphalt. To install it, just unroll the patch, peel the backing off, and apply it to the crack. This type of patch appears to provide a more permanent patch on asphalt slabs than ordinary caulk products, with a reduction in any future cracking.

Holes in asphalt slabs can be filled with cold patches (cold as opposed to the hot asphalt patch seen on paved streets). The cold patch materials are available in twenty-five-pound bags. The patch materials may be dried out and slightly hardened as they come from the bag. Use an electric heat gun to warm and soften the patching material so you can trowel and smooth it.

Using Driveway Sealers

Asphalt Sealers

Asphalt is 95 percent gravel and 5 percent resinous hydrocarbon (oil) binder. If left unsealed, the sunlight will cook the oils out of the asphalt slab, leaving the slab weakened and subject to water penetration. Experts recommend that an asphalt driveway be sealed two or three years after it is laid, and every two years thereafter.

The most common sealers available to

the consumer are latex-based sealers. My own experience has taught me to avoid using the heavier-bodied latex sealers. Frequent, even annual coats of sealer build up quickly and the thick film tends to weather and shrink with surface cracking, called *alligatoring*. Once this cracking occurs the only solution may be to hire a professional contractor to resurface the slab. This is ob-

Peel-and-stick patching strips are available at home centers. Just remove the backing strip and roll the adhesive patch into place.

Asphalt patch products in caulk tubes can be smoothed using a plastic trowel or knife, dipped in mineral spirits.

viously an expensive solution. To avoid the buildup of the thick film of sealer you should use the ordinary—thinner bodied—petroleum-based sealers.

One final tip: Asphalt sealers tend to settle out, with the solids settling to the bottom of the pails. When this settling has occurred it is very difficult to hand-stir the solids into the solution, because the muck at the bottom of the pail is so thick. For this job and many others (mixing wallboard compound, mixing patch plaster or mixing concrete) buy a drywall mixer bit and chuck it into a ½-inch drill to be sure you can thoroughly mix the asphalt sealer. Then pour the sealer on the slab and spread it with the squeegee-broom spreader that is commonly sold with the sealer. Do this on a warm but windless day. Let the sealer set in the sun before application until it is warmed and thinned to a water-like consistency.

Concrete Sealers

It is also important to keep a good sealer coat on concrete slabs. This includes not only the driveway but the garage floor, sidewalks, patio, steps, shop floor and unfinished/unpainted basement floors. Sealing concrete keeps water out on exterior surfaces, and makes the slabs less vulnerable to stains and easier to clean. Finally, unsealed concrete slabs tend to dust on the surface, and walking on the slabs will cause you to track dust throughout the house. If you live in a climate where temperatures are extreme, use a sealer as a barrier to penetration of freezing rain, which can pop the surface on the concrete.

How often should you seal concrete? Pour a bit of water on the slab and watch the water. If it beads up or runs off, the sealer is intact. If the water soaks into the concrete surface the sealer is not working and should be renewed. The best time to make the check or renew the sealer is in the fall, before rain, snow and cold weather combine to attack the slab surface.

To prepare concrete for sealing, use a driveway cleaning product to clean the slab and remove dirt, oil and grease. Such products are available at auto supply stores. Then wash the concrete, using the nozzle on a hose or a pressure-washer to wash away the residue. Let the concrete dry thoroughly, and use a paint roller and an extension handle to apply the sealer. Concrete sealers can be found at building and janitorial supply stores.

CONCRETE

Leveling a Concrete Slab

In the past when a concrete sidewalk, driveway or garage floor sunk or tilted out of level the only solution was to break up and remove the slab, then pour a new one. This obviously was a very expensive undertaking. The good news is that through a process called *mud-jacking*, professionals can now drill injection holes in a concrete slab, pump a concrete slurry (soupy mix) under the slab, and raise it so it is level. This requires expensive equipment, including a ready-mix cement truck, pumps and concrete drills, so it is not a DIY project. But contractors advertise that they can raise most concrete slabs back to level for less than half the cost of removal and replacement. For a bid look in the Yellow Pages under ''Concrete Contractors.''

Repairing Concrete

Use concrete patcher in caulk tubes to fill simple cracks in concrete slabs, steps or block construction. For patching large holes in concrete use one of the concrete patcher kits. The kits contain the cement/sand/gravel mix, plus a latex concrete bonder liquid to bond the new patch material to the old concrete.

To patch a hole or broken edge (such as a step corner) in concrete, first scrub the damaged area with water and a stiff scrub brush to remove all loose material. Then use a nylon brush to apply the concrete bonding liquid to the repair area. Allow the concrete bonder to set before applying the concrete mix.

If the area is on the edge or corner you must make a wood form to hold the concrete in position until it sets firm. For forming the outside corner of the step shown, nail two pieces of scrap wood into a 90-degree angle, and use duct tape to tape the form in place over the corner. With the wooden form in place use a trowel or knife to push the concrete patcher into place in the damaged area. Fill the form as completely as possible to be sure the corner will be square and completely filled.

Allow the concrete patcher to set until it is firm, then carefully remove the form. Use a wet paintbrush to smooth the sides of the patch so the concrete will be smooth. If there are any voids in the patch pick up small amounts of wet concrete and smooth them into place in the voids. Using a fine mist, wet the repair area several times per day, so the concrete has a chance to *cure*, or harden slowly, rather than just dry. Concrete that cures slowly is stronger than concrete that dries rapidly.

Driveway and Concrete Checklist

• Caulk/patch cracks in asphalt driveways. "Bandage" patches are also available for asphalt.

• Fill holes in asphalt slabs with cold patch materials and a heat gun.

• Seal asphalt driveways regularly for longer life.

• Repair concrete cracks with patcher kits. Allow concrete to cure slowly for greater strength.

MAINTAINING THE GARAGE DOOR

As an ex-contractor I believe that most building products do not reach their maximum useful life. Most of the product failures and repair problems I have seen were the result of neglected maintenance. In my experience, one typical victim of neglect is the garage door. Most of the early wood/plywood-panel garage doors fell apart because they suffered water damage on the bottom panel. Although garage doors are

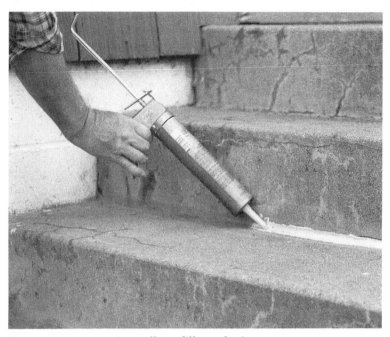

Use concrete repair caulk to fill cracks in concrete. Check the color of the patch. Colors available are white or shades of gray.

now made of aluminum and fiber glass as well as wood, the following advice may be helpful.

First, do not let snow or rain pile or puddle against or under the garage door. The moisture will peel paint, rot wood, cause steel doors to rust, and stain the finish on any type of garage door. New concrete

To patch a broken step corner, clean the repair area to remove dirt and loose concrete. Use a nylon brush to apply latex concrete bonder to the repair area.

Nail two pieces of scrap wood together at a 90-degree (square) angle to make a concrete form. Use duct tape to secure the form in position. Use a trowel or knife to fill the form with concrete.

Let the concrete patch set until firm, then carefully remove the form. Use a wet paintbrush to smooth the surfaces of the patch.

patching materials can now be laid on top of an existing concrete garage floor or apron, forming a slope or curb that will shed water.

Shovel snow away immediately. If snow is left to stand, the sun or solar heat reflected off the door can warm and melt the snow and add to the moisture problem. This can result in a garage door that cannot be opened because it (the door or its bottom weatherstrip) is frozen to the floor or apron. Pour a new layer of concrete on the

floor apron so water will run away. To prevent the bottom weatherstrip or seal on the door from icing and freezing to the floor, spray the seal each fall with a silicone ignition sealer, available from auto repair stores. Or spread a thin layer of petroleum jelly on the vinyl or rubber garage door seal so it won't freeze to the floor.

Using a wrench, check all the nuts and bolts on the door and hardware to be sure nothing has become loose. Lubricate all the moving parts on the garage door hardware to keep the rollers moving freely in the track.

Choose a penetrant/lubricant such as WD-40 or lightweight (10W-20W) motor oil to lubricate the moving parts of the door hardware. This includes the door lock, the inside surface of the track, rollers (shaft and bearings) and the door hinges. Be sure to lubricate anything that moves, including the chain on the garage door opener.

Fixing a Binding Garage Door

If the overhead garage door tends to bind or move unevenly in its tracks, the overhead tracks may be installed incorrectly. If properly installed, the door tracks should be spaced an equal distance apart both where the track makes the bend at the door and at the points where the two tracks are anchored at the back (where the top of the door rests when it is in the top upright position). To check this spacing, have a helper hold a 25-foot measuring tape at the door track, where it begins the bend in the track, while you hold the other end of the tape at the back end of the opposing track. Measure and record this distance between the front and back ends of the two opposing tracks. Now, have the helper hold the tape at the bend on the other track, while you move the other end of the tape to the back end of the opposite track. You have formed the legs of an X with the tape. Check this second measurement: If the two measurements are the same, the tracks are parallel and the door should run

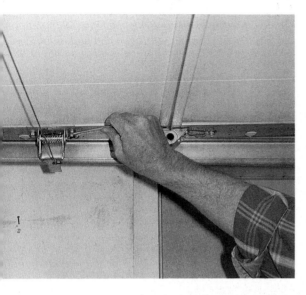

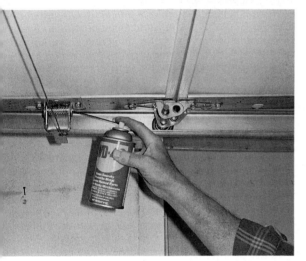

smoothly between them. If one measurement is longer than the other it means the two tracks are not parallel and you must adjust the track anchors until the two tracks are parallel. You should have a helper to make this track adjustment; be careful not to move the tracks so that the door rollers slip out of the track, letting the heavy door fall and injure someone. Make this track adjustment with the door *closed*.

If your overhead garage door is raised and lowered via a spring-and-cable arrangement, you can replace worn or damaged cables quite easily with replacement cables available at most hardware stores and home centers. Remove the old cable and install the new one to match the old. To avoid danger to yourself or damage to the door, do this with the door in the upright position, so the tension is off the door springs and cable.

The other option for the garage door is a coiled spring on a torsion bar, or shaft, above the door. If this coiled torsion spring needs adjustment, do not attempt the repair yourself. The torsion spring is held coiled by an Allen screw or a retaining bolt, and releasing this screw will let the spring uncoil with tremendous force. This can throw the wrench or other tool with bullet-like velocity. Call a professional if the tension needs adjustment on the torsion spring.

(Center, bottom left, below) Use an aerosol lubricant to lubricate anything that moves: hinges, latches, rollers and bearings.

Stanley's Safe-T-Close noncontact sensor (lower right in photo) stops and reverses a closing door if the infrared beam is broken, preventing the door from closing if any object blocks the path of the beam.

Photo courtesy Stanley Home Automation.

Garage Door Safety

Many children have been injured and even killed by faulty garage door openers. Modern openers have safety-reverse systems that are intended to reverse direction if the door should hit any object or person while closing. But this safety-reverse mechanism can fail — without any noticeable change in the door's operation — and can trap and harm a child.

The first step is to warn children not to play with the door opener, and especially to not run under the door while it is moving. Test the opener at least once a month. Place a scrap of wood such as a $2'' \times 4''$ scrap on the floor under the door's path. Close the door and observe the action: When the door touches the scrap of wood the opener should reverse direction and open the door within two seconds. If the safety-reverse feature does not work, you should disconnect the opener and call a repairperson.

MAINTAINING A METAL STORAGE SHED

The average family owns several truckloads of lawn and garden equipment, seasonal sporting goods and tools. The stuff overflows all available storage space; consequently, our backyards are dotted with prefinished metal storage sheds. Judging from their corroded appearance, maintenance for many of those sheds is neglected.

The doors of metal storage sheds open either on hinges or on tracks and rollers. Lubricate the hinges or rollers each spring to keep doors moving freely. Doors with overhead rollers usually have bottom rollers that travel in floor-level tracks. Use a shop vac or a cordless vacuum to clean debris and dirt out of the door track, and lubricate the bottom rollers.

Prefinished metal sheds are sold as "no maintenance" units that need no painting. However, any paint coat eventually will fade and need repainting. Wash the shed as you would aluminum siding. If the shed

Use a cordless vac to clean grit and dirt from the track of the sliding door on the storage shed.

Use a non-greasy lubricant such as the silicone product shown to lubricate the bottom door track on a storage shed.

Garage and Shed Checklist

- Keep moisture from collecting against or under the garage door.
- Check nuts and bolts on the garage door and lubricate moving parts.
- Check garage door tracks for binding or uneven movement; adjust track anchors until parallel.
- Test the safety-reverse feature on garage doors once a month.
- Lubricate tracks and rollers of metal shed doors.
- Treat shed siding according to its material.

Lubricate the rollers and upper door track of the storage shed. Open and close the door several times to distribute the lubricant and ensure doors open smoothly.

REPAIRING AND MAINTAINING A DECK

Adding a deck can greatly increase the living and entertaining capacity of your house, but there is an added penalty in deck maintenance. To ensure that your deck is in good repair and can safely support the load demands of summer activities, be sure to inspect and repair the deck each spring, before the outdoor entertainment season begins.

First, inspect the underside of the deck structure to be sure all beams, joists and posts are in good shape. Visually inspect

is steel and thus subject to rusting, apply a light coat of auto wax to the shed exterior and renew the wax annually. The job will go quickly if you use a buffing wheel (either a rental tool or a buffing wheel and drill) to apply and buff the wax. If the paint becomes badly faded, use odorless mineral spirits to remove the wax from the shed. Then repaint the shed using a top quality acrylic latex house paint.

Use corrosion-proof exterior screws to secure loose deck boards or railing.

Use a heavy duty sander such as this Craftsman sander/grinder to remove old deck finish.

Photo courtesy Sears.

all support framing for signs of insect damage or wood rot. Use an awl or knife point to probe framing. Clues that indicate wood rot or insect infestation include soft wood and easy penetration by the awl or knife. Probe at the bottom and top ends of support posts, where stair treads meet stringers, and where beams and joists are joined. If you find wood rot in one or a few members you can replace those affected members, but if wood rot is widespread the entire deck may need to be rebuilt.

The joist ends may be joined to a ledger joist at the house side of the deck. Usually, the ledger joist is attached to the rim joist of the house with galvanized lag screws. Inspect the lag screws to see if they are tight and are not rusted. Check all joist hangers and other metal connectors to be sure they are rust-free and securely fastened to the ledger joist.

Use a screwdriver to clean any leaves or other debris from between the deck boards. Probe for wood rot at the point where deck boards are fastened to deck joists. If screws or nails are popped or protruding above the deck boards, use a screwdriver or hammer and nail set to drive the fasteners below the surface of the deck boards. Check all steps and railings to be sure they are securely fastened to the deck. Use new fasteners or metal connectors to secure any loose or sagging steps or rails. Remove and replace any deck boards or steps that are badly cracked or warped.

If you prefer the natural look of lumber, use a deck cleaner such as Dekswood to clean the deck, and seal the wood with a clear wood sealer. If you want to stain the wood, use the deck cleaner followed by a penetrating stain. Never use a solid stain or paint to finish a deck, because the solid film of these finishes will quickly show wear patterns in major traffic areas.

MAINTAINING A WOOD RETAINING WALL OR FENCE

Wood structures such as retaining walls and privacy fences can add variety and in-

Use a sponge brush to clean debris from cracks between deck boards and to paint edges of deck boards.

terest to the landscape, but they require periodic attention to keep them looking good and to extend their life. Inspection, maintenance and repair done periodically ensures that you get all the service these structures can deliver.

All exterior woods, whether treated lumber, redwood or cedar, will turn gray if they are left unfinished. This gray color is actually visible dirt or mildew. Use a deck cleaner to clean all unpainted wood structures, and then seal the wood with a clear wood sealer or a penetrating stain to protect the wood from any ultraviolet or moisture damage.

Check the area around the retaining wall or fence for signs of insect infestation. Insects that can destroy wood structures include carpenter ants and termites. Signs of insect problems include seeing the insects around the structure or finding piles of wood residue or sawdust at the base of the structure. If you note carpenter ants near a fence or retaining wall, spray an insecticide such as Ortho's Hornet and Wasp Spray

Add lattice to close bottom of the deck and to prevent windblown rubbish or small animals from getting under the deck.

Photo courtesy Sears.

For cleaning very large or difficult projects, rent a power-washer.

into all cracks or crevices where the insects may be hidden.

If you suspect termite problems check with your local exterminator company for a remedy. Some exterminators will sell chemical insecticides to the DIYer, while some limit service to having their own people apply the insecticide.

Deck and Fence Checklist

• Check posts and beams of decks for rot and insect infestation.

• Clean deck lumber with deck cleaner, and seal with wood sealer or stain with penetrating stain.

• Use deck cleaner on unpainted wood surfaces such as fencing.

• Check around retaining walls and privacy fences for signs of carpenter ants and termites.

Use a deck cleaner and a stiff scrub brush to remove dirt and mildew from retaining wall or other exterior wood projects.

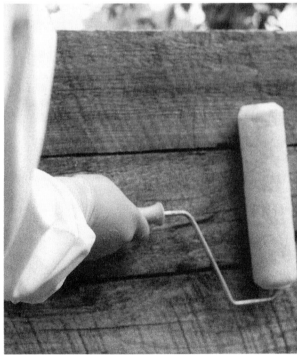

Use a long-nap paint roller to apply a clear wood sealer to your retaining wall or fence.

GLOSSARY

Acoustical Material — Any building material with the ability to reduce sound transmission or reflection. Examples are insulation, tiles and texture spray materials.

Aggregate — Material such as rock or gravel mixed with water and cement to make concrete. Sand and perlite are common aggregates used in texture paints.

Air Space — The cavity formed between building materials in a wall or ceiling. An example would be the space between a pair of studs or rafters enclosed by wallboard on one side and sheathing material on the opposite side.

Angle Iron — L-shaped steel support used to support masonry over a fireplace opening, or to support the load above a window or door.

Attic Ventilators — Roof or gable openings that permit air to circulate. Ventilators may be static, as louvers, or power vents aided by a motor and fan.

Backfill — Excavated earth that is returned to fill the void the excavation created, such as against basement walls, or to fill a trench following construction activity.

Backing — Wood or other material that is installed to provide support for finish materials; i.e., scrap wood installed at corners to provide nailers for wallboard.

Base Shoe — Molding used to cover the crack between the base trim and floor or carpet.

Basement — Lower or support floor of a building; floor that is partially or totally below ground level.

Batt — Material, usually insulation, that is formed into a slab to fit between framing members. Insulation batts may be faced on one side with a vapor barrier of kraft paper or aluminum foil.

Beam — Horizontal support member used to carry a load across a span. A beam is supported on both ends, sometimes with intermediate support posts to the floor, and in turn carries the weight of the floor joists above. Beams are often made of wood: A steel beam may be called an I-beam.

Beam Ceiling — A ceiling in which beams are exposed; they may actually support the roof load but often are added for decorative effect only.

Bearing Wall or Partition — Any wall or partition that supports or *bears* weight from above, as opposed to a nonbearing wall or curtain wall that is a visual or weather barrier supporting no weight but its own.

Bid — A proposal to perform a specified job. The bid should also include *specifications* (also called a *spec sheet*) that spell out the labor, materials and the total price agreed upon.

Blind Nailing — Nails driven so nailheads are not visible. Nails driven at an angle through the tongue of hardwood flooring, so the groove of the adjoining board conceals the nailheads, are blind nailed.

Block — In masonry, refers to a concrete building unit used for building walls. A basement wall may be laid up with mortar and concrete blocks rather than being formed and poured (monolithic) concrete.

Bottom or Sole Plate — The bottom framing member of a wall, usually either 2″ × 4″ or 2″ × 6″. The plate is nailed to the bottom of the studs and to the floor joists or subfloor below it.

Bridging — Wood or steel braces installed in an *X* pattern (diagonally) between floor joists to prevent joists from twisting and to transfer loading between joists.

Building Code — Standards set by a community to ensure safety, strength and value of buildings.

Bundle — Building materials held together

by nylon or steel strapping; bundles are formed for ease of handling and shipping materials, and for easy calculation of contents; a bundle is one-third of a square, or 33 square feet. A square of shingles thus covers 100 square feet of roof.

Carriage — Framing members that support stair steps or treads.

Cement — Powder produced when clay and limestone are burned. When mixed with sand and/or gravel and water it makes concrete.

Center to Center — Distance between two framing members as measured from the center of one to the center of the next; often expressed as *on center* or o.c. The distance between two framing members is usually 16 inches or 24 inches o.c.

Ceramic Tiles — Tiles made of vitreous clay and used as a surface cover or finish on walls, floors or ceilings.

Chalk Line — Tear-shaped metal or plastic container that holds powdered chalk and a strong cord or line. When the line is pulled out it is coated with chalk powder; when held by both ends and snapped over a mark it leaves a line that can be used as a visual or cutting guide.

Cleanout — An opening in plumbing, having a removable cover that one can open to clean the pipe.

Clinch — To drive a nail completely through the lumber so that the tip protrudes on the back side. The tip is then bent over to increase the holding power of the nail.

Combustible/Incombustible — Terms referring to a material's ability to support combustion. Incombustible refers to materials that will not support combustion if subject to house fire temperatures, usually between 1,200° and 1,700° F (648° and 926° C).

Common Wall — The wall that separates two or more apartments, townhouses or condominiums.

Concrete — A mix, usually water/cement/sand/gravel, used for floors, foundations or basement construction.

Conduit — Metal pipe used to route and protect electrical wiring.

Corner Bead — Metal strips formed to a 90-degree angle, nailed on outside corners to provide a strong, straight edge for finishing corners in wallboard construction.

Corner Studs — Wall studs nailed together to form a 90-degree inside corner, as where two walls meet.

Countersink — To sink nails, bolts or screws so that the heads are below the surface of the workpiece.

Courses — Building materials installed in rows or layers; for example, rows of concrete block in a basement wall are called courses.

Cripple — A short framing stud that is cut off to make an opening for a door or window.

Cross Ventilation — Ventilation provided at opposite ends of a room or building, so that moving air can circulate through the entire length of the space. Windows open on opposite sides of a room are said to provide cross ventilation.

Curing — A chemical reaction between water and plaster or cement; hardening.

Curtain Wall — Any wall that does not support weight except its own; a nonbearing wall.

Damp Proof — To coat the exterior side of a concrete wall with cement or asphalt mix so that moisture cannot penetrate the wall.

Dead Load — The weight of all the materials used in the construction of a building, added together, is called the dead load. The live load is the weight of the occupants and furnishings.

Deadening — Materials or building techniques intended to stop noise transfer are called deadening.

Dehumidifier — An appliance designed to reduce the humidity or moisture levels in the air.

Dew Point — Temperature or point at which moisture condenses. In a building the point in a wall or ceiling at which water vapor moisture is inclined to form on the vapor barrier or insulation.

Door Stop — A strip of moulding on the inside or face of a doorframe that stops the door at midpoint on the frame.

Double Header — On bearing walls, the headers over door or window openings must support weight from above, so two header boards are nailed together for extra strength. Double headers are also necessary to support openings cut in floors for stairways.

Downspout — The plastic or metal gutter pipe that carries roof water from the gutter to the ground pipe.

Duct — A round or rectangular pipe, usually made of sheet metal, used to distribute cold or hot air throughout the house.

Efflorescence — White, powdery material that appears on concrete as a result of salts migrating out from inside the concrete mass.

Estimate — An advanced calculation of the cost of a project; may be for materials, labor or both.

Excavate — To remove earth from a basement site or utility trench by means of a bulldozer or backhoe (a backhoe is a tractor with a scoop bucket attached).

Exit — Means or avenue of moving from one part of a building to another part, or for leaving the building for an open space.

False Ceiling — A drop or suspended ceiling, hung on metal or wood grids, to permit covering exposed ducts, pipes or beams.

Feather — To trowel to a thin edge, as when finishing wallboard joints.

Fire Stop — A barrier installed to prevent drafting or spread of fire or flames; may be $2'' \times 4''$ or other blocking installed horizontally between vertical studs.

Fire Wall — A wall of proven fire resistance that is installed between two dwellings (as between townhouses) or between a house and an attached garage. Required by building codes to stop fire from spreading through a building.

Flight — A section of stairs that joins two floors in a house, as a flight of stairs.

Floor Drain — A water drain and trap installed at a low point in the floor so that any water that enters the basement or other area can flow out through main drains into the sewer.

Flush — Even or straight, as a door should be installed flush to the wall.

Footing — The masonry (or wood in wood foundation construction) base that supports the basement walls and the weight of the building above. The footing by code is as thick as the basement wall is thick, and twice as wide as the wall is thick. Thus, a basement built out of 12-inch block would have a footing of poured concrete that is 12 inches thick and 24 inches wide.

Foundation — The masonry, or, lately, wooden structure that is installed between the building and the earth.

Frame — The finish woodwork around a door or window opening.

Framing — The portion of the building that forms the support: studs, joists and rafters are framing.

Frostline — The point in the soil to which frost penetrates in freezing weather. Footings should be built below the frostline, so the earth underneath cannot freeze and heave. This soil depth can be 4 feet (48 inches) in the northern tier of states. Check with the local building department for your frostline depth.

Furring Channel — The horizontal support in the grid that holds a suspended ceiling.

Grade — The slope of the ground surface around a house, established so the lawn slopes away from the foundation.

Ground Floor — The floor of a house that is at or near the finished grade.

Grout — Mortar or other filler used to fill joints between masonry or ceramic tiles.

Gutter — Metal or fiber glass channel that is installed at the house eaves to collect rain from the roof and direct it to the ground.

Gypsum — Optional term that refers to wallboard; more specifically the plaster core between the two layers of paper on a wallboard panel.

H-Beam — Steel support beam placed

down the middle of a basement to hold the floor joists; called an *H*-beam or *I*-beam, depending on the width of the top and bottom flanges.

Head Room — Vertical space between the floor and ceiling, stairs and ceiling (in a stairway), or between the floor and header on a door opening.

Header — Horizontal lumber support that is installed over the top of door or window openings. The header supports the weight of the roof and framing, or of the floor above.

Insulation Board — Panels, usually measuring $4' \times 8'$, that provide insulation value. May be fiberboard or beadboard (made of Styrofoam beads).

Insulation — Any material that provides a barrier to passage of heat, electricity or sound.

Jamb — Material that surrounds or cases a window or door opening. Top, horizontal piece is called the *head jamb*; vertical pieces at both sides are *side jambs*.

Joint Cement — Material available in powder (to be mixed with water) or in paste form (ready-mixed) used for finishing joints in wallboard construction. Also called *mud* (by pros), taping compound or taping cement.

Joist — Parallel framing members, spaced 16 inches or 24 inches on center, that support either the floor or ceiling.

Joist Hanger — Metal device, shaped like a *U*, used to connect two joists or a joist and a beam at right angles to each other.

Lag Screw — A wood screw that has a head like a bolt, driven with a wrench rather than a screwdriver.

Laminate — (1) Act of joining two workpieces together using adhesive. (2) The finish material known as plastic laminate used in cabinet and furniture construction.

Landing — A platform that joins or terminates a flight of stairs.

Lath — Base material for plaster or stucco; can be wood, gypsum or steel (wire).

Level — Tool used to establish horizontal or vertical (plumb) lines.

Live Load — Weight of materials that are not part of the house, as furniture and appliances; also weight (combined) of occupants of a house; as opposed to *dead load*, the weight of the house itself.

Lock Set — Complete set of hardware including the lock, knobs, screws and strike plate.

Masonry — Term that encompasses concrete or tile materials used in construction.

Mastic — Coating or adhesive material often used in reference to ceramic tile adhesive or vinyl adhesive for tile or sheet goods.

Matched Joint — Wood joint that is closely fitted, either with glue or with tongue-and-groove joinery.

Mechanical Equipment — All devices installed by the "mechanical trades," i.e., electrical, plumbing, heating and air conditioning materials and equipment.

Mesh — Metal wire reinforcing base for plaster or concrete.

Moisture Barrier — Any material (usually building paper or polyethylene plastic sheets) used to block the flow of moisture or vapor through walls, ceilings or floors.

Nail Pops — Also called *fastener failure*, is also common in screw application of wallboard. Caused by shrinkage of framing members after wallboard is applied. Prevention: To avoid popped nails in wallboard, siding or sheathing use dry lumber and construction adhesives.

Nonbearing Wall — Wall or partition that provides a curtain or barrier to passage, but does not support any structural load.

Oakum — Filler, usually rope material soaked in tar, used to fill joints or caulk between materials. Available at plumbing supply stores, as plumber's oakum, used to fill bell housing on drainpipes.

Offset — Ledge or recess where there is a change in material or wall thickness.

On Center (O.C.) — To avoid confusion the interval between framing members such as studs, joists or rafters is always expressed as *on center*, or O.C., rather than *between*. The measurement refers to the distance from the center of one framing member to the center of the next.

Parging — Coat of mortar, usually cement, applied to damp-proof concrete basement walls. The material is troweled on the outside of the wall.

Parquet — Small squares of wood applied to the floor or other surface in a pattern.

Perm Factor — Rate at which moisture or vapor moves through a wall or ceiling and each or all of its components — framing, wallboard, vapor barrier, sheathing, etc.

Perpendicular — Measurement or material as seen straight up and down or plumb, as opposed to side to side or horizontal.

Pier — Base, usually concrete or treated wood, that supports posts or other loads.

Plan — Horizontal section drawing of a house that shows size, shape, location of doors, windows, walls and equipment.

Plaster Board — Optional term used to refer to wallboard, gypsum board.

Plate, Sill — The flat framing member, usually a $2'' \times 6''$ or $2'' \times 8''$, that is bolted to the foundation and is a base for the rim joists around the perimeter of the foundation or basement wall.

Post — Timber or metal pipe placed on end to support any load above it.

Prefinished — Refers to building components that are delivered to the buyer with the finish already applied at the factory: Flooring, cabinets, paneling and siding are examples.

Prehung Door — A door that is purchased as an assembled unit, already installed with hinges in a frame and prebored to receive the lockset.

Putty — Pliable filler material used to fill wood holes or to seal glass in a window; also plumber's putty, used around sink rims, etc.

Quarter Round — Wood moulding that describes a 90-degree arc, or quarter of a circle.

R Value — The *R* stands for "resistance" to heat flow, and is a means of measuring the value of materials used for thermal insulation.

Rock Wool — Insulation made from silica or other rock material.

Rough Hardware — Hardware or fasteners used in framing, such as nails, bolts or lag screws.

Roughing In — The preliminary or first stage of the work: For plumbing, for example, roughing in is the term for routing all supply and waste pipes to their locations, ready for fixture installation.

Scab — A short piece of lumber placed so it bridges the joint between two pieces of lumber that are laid out with a butt joint. The scab is then fastened so it connects the two pieces of lumber.

Scribing — Marking and cutting wood or other material so its edge matches the surface it butts against, as the edge of a cabinet or paneling against a wall.

Section — Sometimes called a *through section*, an illustration that shows a structure in cross section.

Shim — A piece of wood, often a wood shingle with a wedge shape, placed to level or plumb cabinets, doorframe or windows.

Shoe Molding — A molding strip that covers the crack between the baseboard and the floor.

Sleeper — A sort of furring strip for floors; a wood strip that is embedded in or fastened to a concrete or wood floor to provide nailers or leveling as needed.

Soffit — Soffits, sometimes called *drop ceilings*, are the underside of eaves (exterior) or the lowered area above cabinets in a kitchen or bath.

Soil Stack — The vertical drainpipe that provides waste flow downward and ventilation upward through the roof.

Sound Transmission — Usually expressed in decibels as the unit of measurement; the sound that passes through a given material or building unit.

Spalling — Deterioration of the face of a masonry surface, usually caused by moisture or frost problems.

Span — The distance separating supporting members such as beams or bearing walls.

Specifications — A detailed list that shows

the size and quality or brand of materials to be used in construction.

STC — Sound Transmission Class; relates, via decibel loss, how well a building unit resists sound passage.

Stringer — A support for joists or other framing members; in stairs, the members that support the steps or treads.

Stud — The framing members that support the walls, to which the wallboard is fastened on the inside and sheathing/siding is fastened on the outside.

Subfloor — The first or primary layer of wood that covers the top of the floor joists.

Suspended Ceiling — A ceiling usually supported by wires and hung beneath the level of the joists. Suspended ceilings are often chosen where pipes, ducts or framing prevent installation of a level ceiling at the bottom of rafters or joists.

Taping — The term used in wallboard construction that refers to the entire process of finishing wallboard, including sealing the joints with wallboard tape and applying two trowel coats that level the joints.

Template — A full-sized pattern, often cut from builder's paper and used for layout purposes. Also, an adjustable tool used to mark hinge locations on a door edge, called a *hinge template*.

Total Run — The overall horizontal measurement of a stair.

Underlayment — Material used as a base for applying some finish material, as carpet underlayment.

Vanity — The base cabinet or counter in a bathroom.

Vapor Barrier — A barrier, usually aluminum foil, kraft paper or polyethylene plastic, that is installed in the warm side of a wall, ceiling or floor to slow moisture or vapor penetration. Also serves as a barrier to air infiltration.

Wallboard — Panels consisting of a plaster core and front and back covers of paper, used for interior finish in place of plaster. Often called *plaster board* or *Sheetrock*, which is a trade name.

Working Drawings — Detailed project drawings that provide a guide for construction.

LIFE EXPECTANCIES OF BUILDING MATERIALS

There are two cost factors to consider when buying a house. The first is the initial price of the house. But the second and more important cost is the cost of living in and maintaining the house. While there is not much you can do about the cost of a building plot, prevailing wages or contractor's profits, you can do a lot to control the cost of living in the house. The key is simply to buy materials and components with future repair and maintenance in mind. While many of us are forced by our budgets to shop for prices, buying quality materials can play an important role in reducing any future home maintenance and repair requirements.

Someone has said that true happiness is to own nothing that needs to be painted, washed or watered. That is a difficult goal for anyone who owns a house. In fact, it may often seem that in buying a house you actually bought a second job, where something always needs to be done.

But as you repair and remodel the house keep in mind that aluminum and vinyl siding will need only an annual washing. Windows and doors are now available with prefinished exterior cladding that will need no scraping or painting until the mortgage has been paid. Asphalt shingles are now available with thirty-year warranties, and metal,

concrete or tile roofing can last for several lifetimes.

If you buy quality, even small repair and maintenance items can save you time and money. For example, quality paint and wall or floor coverings not only will look richer but will last longer. Quality does not cost; it pays. Remember too that the labor costs are the same, whether you are installing quality or bargain materials.

Knowing the expected lifespan of various building components can also save you money. How much longer will the eight-year-old roof last? Is it time to replace the ten-year-old water heater? Is it worthwhile repairing a six-year-old clothes dryer, or is it time to replace it? Knowing the answers to these questions can be a valuable aid. If you doubt the honesty of a contractor who advises you to replace your garbage disposal or your gas-fired forced-air furnace, consult the following charts. If you don't know how often you should paint your siding or replace your roof shingles, the charts can be a valuable reference. But keep in mind that the chart lists average expected lifespans: If you always buy quality you can extend these numbers to the maximum. The charts were compiled by Dean Christ and are shown here with his permission.

Item	Useful Life	Remarks
Footings and foundations		
Footings	life	First three items are likely to last up to 250
Foundation	life	years. There are homes in the United
Concrete block	life	States over 300 years old. Structural defects
Waterproofing:		that do develop are a result of poor soil
Bituminous coating	5 years	conditions.
Pargeting with Ionite	life	
Termite-proofing	5 years	Maybe earlier in damp climates.
Gravel outside	30-40 years	Depends on usage.
Cement block	life	Less strong than concrete block.
Rough structure		
Floor system (basement)	life	
Framing exterior walls	life	Usually plaster directly on masonry. Plaster is solid and will last forever. Provides tighter seal than drywall and better insulation.
Framing interior walls	life	In older homes, usually plaster on wood lath. Lath strips lose resilience, causing waves in ceilings and walls.
Concrete work:		
Slab	life	(200 years)
Precast decks	10-15 years	
Precast porches	10-15 years	
Site-built porches and steps	20 years	
Sheet metal		
Gutter, downspouts, and flashing:		
Aluminum	20-30 years	Never requires painting, but dents and pits. May need to be replaced sooner for appearance.
Copper	life	Very durable and expensive. Requires regular cleaning and alignment.
Galvanized iron	15-25 years	Rusts easily and must be kept painted every 3 to 4 years.

Item	Useful Life	Remarks
Rough electrical		
Wiring:		
Copper	life	
Aluminum	life	
Romex	life	
Circuit-breaker		
Breaker panel	30-40 years	
Individual breaker	25-30 years	
Rough plumbing		
Pressure pipes:		
Copper	life	Strongest and most common. Needs no maintenance.
Galvanized iron	30-50 years	Rusts easily and is major expense in older homes. Most common until 1940.
Plastic	30-40 years	
Waste pipe:		
Concrete	20 years	
Vitreous china	25-30 years	
Plastic	50-70 years	Usage depends upon soil conditions. Acid soils can eat through plastic.
Cast iron	life	
Lead	life	A leak cannot be patched. If bathroom is remodeled, lead must be replaced.
Heating and venting		
Duct work:		
Galvanized	50-70 years	
Plastic	40-60 years	Type used depends upon climate.
Fiberglass	40-60 years	
AC rough-in		Same as Duct work
Roof		
Asphalt shingles	15-25 years	Most common. Deterioration subject to climate. Granules come off shingles. Check downspouts.
Wood shingles and shakes	30-40 years	Expensive. Contracts and expands due to climate.
Tile	30-50 years	Tendency to crack on sides.
Slate	life	High quality. Maintenance every 2 to 3 years as nails rust.
Metal	life	Shorter life if allowed to rust.
Built-up asphalt	20-30 years	Maintenance required — esp. after winter

Item	Useful Life	Remarks
Roof, cont'd		
Felt	30-40 years	
Tar and gravel	10-15 years	
Asbestos shingle	30-40 years	Shingles get brittle when walked on. Maintenance every 1 to 3 years.
Composition shingles	12-16 years	
Tin	life	Will rust easily if not kept painted regularly. Found a lot in inner-city row houses.
4 or 5 built-up ply	15-25 years	Layers of tar paper on tar.
Masonry		
Chimney	life	
Fireplace	20-30 years	
Fire brick	life	
Ash dump	life	
Metal fireplace	life	
Flue tile	life	
Brick veneer	life	Joints must be pointed every 5 to 6 years.
Brick	life	
Stone	life	Unless a porous grade stone like limestone.
Block wall	life	
Masonry floors	life	Must be kept waxed every 1 to 2 years.
Stucco	life	Requires painting every 8 to 10 years. More susceptible to cracking than brick. Replacement is expensive. Maintenance cycles for all types of masonry structures, including those found in urban areas, subjected to dirt, soot, and chemicals: Caulking — every 20 years Pointing — every 35 years Sandblasting — every 35 years
Windows and doors		
Window glazing	5-6 years	
Storm windows and gaskets	life	Aluminum and wood.
Screen doors	5-8 years	
Storm doors	10-15 years	
Interior doors (lauan)	10 years	
Sliding doors	30-50 years	
Folding doors	30-40 years	
Sliding screens	30 years	

Item	Useful Life	Remarks
Windows and doors, cont'd		
Garage doors	20-25 years	Depends upon initial placement of springs, tracks, and rollers.
Steel casement windows	40-50 years	Have leakage and condensation problems. Installed mostly in 1940s and 1950s.
Wood casement windows	40-50 years	Older types very drafty.
Jalousie	30-40 years	Fair quality available in wood and aluminum. Used mostly for porches.
Wood double-hung windows	40-50 years	
Insulation		
Foundation	life	
Roof, ceiling	life	
Roof -- electric vent -- automatic	10-15 years	
Walls	life	
Floor	life	
Weatherstripping:		
Metal	8-9 years	
Plastic gasket	5-8 years	
Exterior trim		
Wood siding	life	Must be kept painted regularly -- every 5-7 years.
Metal siding	life	May rust due to climate.
Aluminum siding	life	Maintenance free if baked-on finish.
Shutters:		
Wood	20 years	
Metal	20-30 years	
Plastic	life	
Aluminum	life	
Posts and columns	life	
Gable vents:		
Wood	10-14 years	
Aluminum	life	
Gable vent screens	Same as gable vents	
Cornice and rake trim	life	
Trellis	20 years	Will rot in back even if painted because of moisture.
Exterior paint		
Wood	3-4 years	Climate a strong factor.
Brick	3-4 years	
Aluminum	10-12 years	

Item	Useful Life	Remarks
Exterior paint, cont'd		
Gutters, downspouts, and flashing:		
Aluminum	10-12 years	
Copper	life	No painting required.
Stairs		
Stringer	50 years	
Risers	50 years	
Treads	50 years	
Baluster	50 years	
Rails	30-40 years	
Starting levels	50 years	
Disappearing stairs	30-40 years	
Drywall and plaster		
Drywall	40-50 years	Lifetime is adequately protected by exterior walls and roof. Cracks must be regularly spackled.
Plaster	life	Thicker and more durable than drywall. Exterior must be properly maintained.
Ceiling suspension	life	
Acoustical ceiling	life	
Luminous ceiling	10-20 years	Discolors easily.
Ceramic tile		
Tub alcove and shower stall	life	Proper installation and maintenance required for long life. Cracks appear due to moisture and joints; must be grouted every 3-4 years.
Bath wainscote	life	
Ceramic floor	life	
Ceramic tile	life	
Finish carpentry		
Baseboard and shoe	40-50 years	
Door and window trim	40-50 years	
Wood paneling	40-50 years	
Closet shelves	40-50 years	
Fireplace mantel	30-40 years	
Flooring		
Oak floor	life	In most older homes, first story floor is oak; second and third story floors are hard pine.
Pine floor	life	
Slate flagstone floor	40-50 years	
Resilient (vinyl)	10-15 years	Because of scuffing may have to be replaced earlier.
Terrazzo	life	
Carpeting	5-8 years	Standard carpeting.

Item	Useful Life	Remarks
Cabinets and vanities		
Kitchen cabinets	18-30 years	
Bath vanities	18-30 years	
Countertop	18-30 years	
Medicine cabinets	15-20 years	
Mirrors	10-15 years	
Tub enclosures	18-25 years	
Shower doors	18-25 years	
Bookshelves	life	Depends on wood used.
Interior painting		
Wall paint	3-5 years	
Trim and door	3-5 years	
Wallpaper	3-7 years	
Electrical finish		
Electric range and oven	12-20 years	
Vent hood	15-20 years	
Disposal	5-12 years	
Exhaust fan	8-10 years	
Water heater	10-12 years	
Electric fixtures	20-30 years	
Doorbell and chimes	8-10 years	
Fluorescent bulbs	3-5 years	
Plumbing finish		
Dishwasher	5-15 years	
Gas water heater	8-12 years	
Gas refrigerator	15-25 years	
Toilet seats	8-10 years	
Commode	15-25 years	
Steel sinks	15-20 years	
China sinks	15-20 years	
Faucets	life	Washers must be replaced frequently.
Flush valves	18-25 years	
Well and septic system	15-30 years	Depends on soil and rock formations.
Hot water boilers	30-50 years	Becomes increasingly inefficient with age and may have to be replaced before it actually breaks down.
Heating finish		
Wall heaters	12-17 years	
Warm air furnaces	25-30 years	Most common today.

Item	Useful Life	Remarks
Heating finish, cont'd		
Radiant heating:		
Ceiling	20-30 years	
Baseboard	20-40 years	
AC unit	8-18 years	
AC compressors	10-18 years	Regular maintenance required.
Humidifier	7-8 years	
Electric air cleaners	8-10 years	
Appliances		
Refrigerator	15-25 years	
Washer	8-12 years	
Dryer	8-12 years	
Combo washer and dryer	7-10 years	
Garage door opener	8-10 years	
Disposal units	8-12 years	
Dishwasher	8-12 years	
Lawn mower	7-10 years	Must be serviced regularly.
Vacuum cleaner	6-10 years	
Music system (intercom)	30-40 years	
Appointments		
Closet rods	life	
Blinds	10-15 years	
Drapes	5-10 years	
Towel bars	10-15 years	
Soap grab	10-12 years	
Others		
Fences and screens	20-30 years	
Splash blocks	6-7 years	
Patios (concrete)	15-50 years	
Gravel walks	3-5 years	
Concrete walks	10-25 years	
Sprinkler system	15-25 years	
Asphalt driveway	5-6 years	With patchwork may last 15-20 years.
Tennis court	20-40 years	

The chart above was compiled by Dean Christ and is used here courtesy of the Economics Division, National Association of Home Builders.

APPENDIX 2

RESOURCES

Emerson Electric Co.
9797 Reavis Road
St. Louis, MO 63123
 Electronic air cleaner

The Flood Company
Hudson, OH 44236-0399
(800) 321-3444
 Dekswood deck cleaner, Penetrol paint
 conditioner

San-Teen Products
1321 7th Street So.
Hopkins, MN 55423
 San-Teen drain cleaner

Thoro System Products
7800 NW 38th Street
Miami, FL 33166-6599
 Stucco finish

Whirlpool Corp.
(800) 253-1301
 Electric stove element dressing, polishing
 cleaner

INDEX